INSTRUCTOR'S MANUAL

FOUNDATION PRESS

ENVIRONMENTAL
LAW AND POLICY

THIRD EDITION

By

LESLIE KAUFFMAN
LEAP Publishing Services, Inc.

CONCEPTS AND INSIGHTS SERIES®

FOUNDATION PRESS
2010

THOMSON REUTERS

© 2010 By THOMSON REUTERS/FOUNDATION PRESS

      195 Broadway, 9th Floor

      New York, NY 10007

      Phone Toll Free 1–877–888–1330

      Fax (212) 367–6799

      foundation-press.com

Printed in the United States of America

ISBN 978–1–59941–773–8

mat #40891047

PART I

Tools of the Trade

CHAPTER 1
An Introduction to Environmental Law and Policy

I.   Why Study Environmental Law?

What is environmental law and policy?
- Simplest definition:
  - The use of governmental authority to protect the natural environment and human health from the impacts of pollution and development.

Major flaws in the definition:
- Not exciting
- Doesn't explain why environmental law matters

Justification for studying environmental law and policy:
- Consistently newsworthy
- Influences how and where we live
- Will affect our children and future generations

Relevant issues include:
- Resource development vs. endangered animal; plant protection vs. potential pollution
- Community economic development vs. endangered animal; plant protection vs. potential pollution
- Political implications vs. endangered animal; plant protection v. potential pollution

Example: Oil drilling in Alaska brings economic development to impoverished Eskimo communities and lessens America's dependence on foreign oil; however, it poses a slight risk of polluting a natural land area and may impact animals indigenous to the area.

Environmental law is often viewed as a combination of pollution law and natural resources law. While these are actually two distinct areas, Chapter 2 will examine the fundamental similarities of these areas.

Suggested Discussion Questions and Activities

1. How does the environment affect individuals?
2. How do individuals (the students) affect the environment?
3. What role should the federal and state governments have in preserving the environment?
4. How can the federal and state governments truly balance the interests of private property owners and the public's right to use public property?
5. Do any students utilize public property to bike, hunt, fish, off road, or other activity? If so, have them relate what this activity means to them and how their lives might be different without these opportunities.
6. Have any students ever been directly affected by an environmental problem? If so, have them describe the problem and have the class discuss the severity of the problem, how it might have been prevented, and who was to blame.

II.   A Short History of Environmental Protection

A.   *Natural Resources*

Wilderness has always been special for Americans.

Wilderness has also become big business in terms of tourism.
- Wilderness excursions
  - Sales of high-tech gear
  - Jobs for guides and other expedition company employees
- Fascination with family-friendly rides and attractions

Our fascination and love affair with the wilderness is, however, quite recent.
- For much of the past two millennia, the wilderness was viewed as inhospitable, dangerous, and an affront to civilization.
  - Adam and Eve were banished to the wilderness for eating the forbidden fruit.
  - Moses and the tribes of Israel wandered the wilderness for forty years after their exodus from Egypt.
  - Jesus Christ was tempted by the devil for forty days in the wilderness.
  - Hansel and Gretel were lost in a forest described as a place of monstrous beasts and creatures.
  - The area around the colony at Plymouth was described as "hideous and desolate" leading the Pilgrims to seek to "civilize" the wilderness.

Early Americans sought not to convert the wilderness into cities but to make it a controlled and manageable rural ground.
- Thomas Jefferson considered the rural farmers of America to be its ideal citizens.

1-2

Westward expansion's primary obstacle and goal was to tame the wilderness.

- Settlement in wilderness areas required clearing of the land and making it able to sustain crops.
  - ○ "A stump was our symbol of progress" *naturalist Aldo Leopold (1930)*
- Expansion also brought a broad appreciation of wilderness.
  - ○ Poetry
  - ○ Art
  - ○ Novels
  - ○ Other writings

The most notable Transcendentalist was Henry David Thoreau, who wrote, "In Wildness is the preservation of the world," espousing the view that modern industrial society was cutting them off from God by cutting people off from nature.

Thoreau's Transcendentalist view was not widely accepted and federal policy was intent on populating wilderness areas with those willing to transform and farm the land.

- The Homestead Act of 1862 (along with other statutes) provided, free of charge, millions of acres of land to those willing to live on and farm the land.
- Cattle were allowed to freely graze on public grasslands.
- Miners were granted exclusive control of minerals found on public lands.
- Railroads were granted free land to increase westward expansion.

To offset the total conversion of public land to private ownership, the federal government began the creation of national reservations and parks.

- Arkansas Hot Springs was the first in 1832.
- Yosemite Valley was granted to California in 1864 as a park "for public use, resort and recreation."
- Yellowstone Park was created in 1872 "as a public park, or pleasuring ground for the benefit and enjoyment of the people."

These, and other acts, were not entirely benevolent, nor aesthetically or culturally based. Arkansas Hot Springs was created primarily to counteract the commercial exploitation of its geysers, and New York's Adirondacks Forest Reserve, created in 1885, was done primarily to ensure a clean water source for New York City.

Preservationists and conservationists were thrust into prominence during the debate over the Hetch Hetchy Valley debate regarding Yosemite National Park. A movement was made to dam the Tuolomne River in the Hetch Hetchy Valley. Proponents of the dam argued that the project would increase San Francisco's water and electricity supply, while preservationists argued that the damming of the river would destroy the beauty of the valley. Despite an effective and spirited campaign by the preservationists, led by John Muir, the river was dammed. Nevertheless, preservationists gained stature and legitimacy during the process, popularizing the wilderness ethic.

Following World War II, America experienced significant growth of its middle class. This corresponded with the construction of an interstate highway system. Interest in America's public lands grew, as did the number of conservationist groups.

During the Hetch Hetchy Valley controversy, only a handful of conservationist groups existed; however, by the early 1950s, there were over 300. When a dam was proposed in Colorado's Echo Park that would have threatened Dinosaur National Monument, a grassroots letter writing campaign was organized, unlike any seen before, and the project was abandoned after a five-year debate.

Environmental groups continued to lobby Congress, and a variety of landmark laws were enacted:
- Wilderness Act of 1964
- Land and Water Conservation Act of 1965
- National Historic Preservation Act of 1966
- National Wild and Scenic Rivers System Act in 1968

These new acts stressed the retention and preservation of public lands halting the move toward disposal of these lands and conversion to private ownership.

The 1970s saw the passage of laws designed to preserve environmentally important lands that were privately owned.
- Endangered Species Act of 1973
- Clean Water Act of 1972, amended in 1977 to protect wetlands

While these and other laws frequently make environmentalists and private landowners adversaries, the laws do create important protections, ensuring biodiversity and preservation of expendable resources and endangered wildlife.

Suggested Discussion Questions and Activities
1. How might the history of America be different had the federal government not encouraged westward expansion?
2. Do any of the students believe that they would have had the "pioneer spirit" to head into the unknown wilderness to build a new life?
3. How and why did the conclusion of World War II affect the public perception of environmental policy?
4. Have students do research to find a federal and/or state statute related to this chapter and discuss its provisions and ramifications either orally or in writing.
5. Break the students into two groups and have each side advocate a position regarding the Hetch Hetchy Valley controversy.

B.   *Pollution*

Pollution has been an issue since the rise of farms and cities in previously unsettled areas.
- Dilution was a manageable control when population densities were low and organic wastes could simply assimilate into the surrounding environment.

- The rise in the number of cities along with the growing size of cities made dilution largely ineffective.
  o Organic waste grew in volume.
  o Industrial waste was introduced.
  o Air pollution became problematic.
- The proliferation of pollutants became a noticeable health hazard.
  o In London as early as 1306, citizens were threatened with "grievous ransoms" for air pollution, and in 1346 were fined for not removing waste from outside their homes.
  o The Chicago River often congealed from slaughterhouse runoff.

Nevertheless, anti-pollution statutes largely did not exist.

Common law actions in trespass and nuisance were used to address pollution issues.

Following World War II, the use of synthetics and pesticides grew and additional pollution problems grew.

The event that brought public attention to the issue of pollution and galvanized the movement to reform the laws and control the problem was the publication of Rachel Carson's 1962 book, *Silent Spring*, which documented the dangers of DDT.
- This publication led to President Kennedy's formation of advisory groups to examine the issues of pesticide use and control, which in turn led to increased Congressional scrutiny.
- *Silent Spring* generated enormous interest and concern, giving rise to numerous advocacy-based organizations.

Advocacy groups became so organized and influential that in *Scenic Hudson Preservation Conference v. Federal Power Commission*, Scenic Hudson became the first environmental group to be granted standing to bring suit.

Environmental issues became a prominent political issue in the 1970s:
- Over 20 million people participated in the first Earth Day in 1970.
- The Environmental Protection Agency was created in 1970.
- Clean Water Act of 1972
- Resource Conservation and Recovery Act of 1976
- The 1972 presidential primary election between President Richard Nixon and Senator Edmund Muskie featured a particular effort by both candidates to court the "environmental vote."

Events such as New York's Love Canal and Pennsylvania's Three Mile Island incident have kept the environmental issue in the public consciousness.

The laws proliferated in the 1970s were certainly not perfect. They did establish a basis for amendments and new statutes which have greatly strengthened and solidified modern environmental law policies and protections.

Public opinion and awareness is also prominent as recent public opinion polls show that approximately 80 percent of respondents consider themselves to be "environmentalists."

Suggested Discussion Questions and Activities

1. Explain or have the students research the Love Canal and Three Mile Island events and discuss the environmental implications of each.
2. Explain or have the students research the nuclear meltdown at Chernobyl and discuss how a similar end result in Pennsylvania at Three Mile Island would have affected the east coast and the United States as a whole.
3. How and why did administrative law grow in the area of pollution control?
4. Why, or why isn't, the protection of endangered wildlife important? If students argue that preserving endangered species is not a worthy endeavor, ask if their opinion would be different if the endangered animal were a dog or cat.
5. Should it matter whether endangered wildlife is an animal or a plant species?
6. What is the importance of the standing ruling in *Scenic Hudson Preservation Conference v. Federal Power Commission*? Do the students agree with the ruling?
7. Assign, or have the students choose, an animal or plant species and do research and report on the animal's significance in the food chain and the effect the extinction of the animal would have on nature. Assigning exotic (elephants, rhinoceroses) or seemingly insignificant animal (ants, flies, snakes) or plant life (grass, kelp) would work best.

C.   *Where Are We Today? The Obama Administration and Environmental Protection*

Environmental law underwent constant change throughout the 1970s and 1980s.

Growing partisanship over environmental issues, however, slowed the pace of new federal legislation in the late 1990s and the first years of the 20th century. The result has been legislative stagnation.

- For example, Congress refused to ratify the Kyoto Protocol or address issues of climate change.
- Since the 1990s, there have been few significant amendments to major federal environmental legislation.
  - 1992 Clean Air Act Amendments
  - 1996 Food Quality Protect Act
  - 1996 Safe Drinking Water Act Amendments

Upon taking office in January 2009, President Barack Obama promised a renewed focus on environmental issues.

- Energy is a main focus—Obama hopes to expand the use of solar and wind energy.
- Obama also has also advocated for legislation to limit U.S. emissions of greenhouse gases.

- The Obama Administration has also taken action to increase federal environmental protection in a wide variety of areas.

It remains unclear if the Obama Administration will be able to carry out its ambitious environmental agenda.

- Republicans—and some Democrats—in Congress strongly oppose Obama's legislative goals as too costly or ill conceived.
- Some environmental groups, by contrast, complain that the administration is not moving quickly enough.

Suggested Discussion Questions and Activities

1. How do students feel about the relative lack of environmental legislation in the United States since the 1980s? Do they believe that further environmental protections are needed? If so, how do they explain the unwillingness of Congress to push for such protections?
2. Assign, or have students choose, one of the environmental proposals of the Obama Administration and ask students to research and report on where it currently stands. What compromises, if any, have been made to the legislation? Has the legislation passed through Congress? Why or why not?

PART I
Tools of the Trade

CHAPTER 2
Perspectives on Environmental Law and Policy

I.   Basic Themes of Environmental Law

One cannot intelligently apply the law to an environmental issue without examining and understanding the forces that have created the problem.

Forces and matters to be considered include:
- Climate change
- Development affecting species habitat
- Air quality and pollution
- Water quality and pollution
- Societal concerns

A.   Scientific Uncertainty

Scientific uncertainty is frequently the defining feature of environmental policy.

Technical and economic issues pertaining to economic policy are almost always an issue; however, lawmakers rarely have perfect information when making policy.

Example I: Global Warming
- Will increases in the earth's temperature increase cloud formation?
- What has been the true cause of increased measured temperatures over the past century?
    - o Increased carbon emissions?
    - o An unrelated warming trend?
    - o A combination of factors?
- What costs might global warming cause?

Example II: Pesticides
- Causes cancer in mice
    - o Tests involve relatively high exposure levels used in tests.
- No credible baseline data pertaining to cancer causation in humans
    - o Human everyday level of exposure is at a significantly lower level.
- Human beings and mice are obviously significantly different in size and weight.

Nevertheless, decisions must be made *today* as the answers to the questions in the above examples are sought.

Land development produces a number of difficult questions:
- If a species of animal is affected, how much of land set aside would be enough to preserve the species and habitat?
- Is the change in habitat the true cause of the species endangerment, or might natural cause, such as predators, be the issue?

Environmental problems can rarely be attributed to a single or isolated cause.
- Example: What is causing salmon stock depletion in the Pacific Northwest?
  - Overfishing?
  - River damming?
  - Logging?
  - Industry pollution along the waterways?
  - Over-reliance on hatchery fish?

Is it one of these? Two? Three? All of them? If only one or two potential causes are regulated and controlled, will the problem be rectified?

Problem-causing actions are frequently very difficult to quantify.
- Example: Exactly how much did an individual coal burning facility in the Ohio Valley contribute to an acid rain occurrence in New York?
  - How can this be accurately measured?

Consider the global warming controversy:
- Industry-sponsored advocates urge more research prior to action.
  - Costs to change current practices may beget additional future costs that may have been unnecessary.
- Industry opponents argue that waiting for scientific certainty may delay action until it is too late.

Strategies to alleviate much of the debate:
- Develop better information from the onset
- Adopt a precautionary principle strategy
  - Caution in the face of significant but uncertain threats
  - Internationally, this advocates the shift of the burden of proof regarding offending actions from those challenging practices to those who seek to engage in a practice.

Suggested Discussion Questions and Activities
1. Have the students debate how much information needs to be acquired and verified before an environmental policy decision can, or should, be made.

2. With regard to the precautionary principle approach, can we really trust industry to self-monitor? Assuming that oversight was required, what would need to be implemented in order to scrutinize and verify self-monitoring data? Can this be done on an international level?

B.   Market Failures

Misaligned incentives underlie most environmental conflicts.

There is an inevitable balancing of the economic expectations of the individual with the reinforcement of environmental protection policies.
- What is the individual's reward structure?
- What is the benefit to society by protecting the environment?
- Are there specific laws and penalties for violation that apply to the situation?

The ultimate task for an environmental lawyer is to strike a reasonable and acceptable balance satisfying the law, society, and the individuals they represent.

Environmentally-friendly practices frequently result in increased industry costs.
- The supply- and demand-driven market does not always result in sound environmental practices being required by the public.

Suggested Discussion Question
1. Assume that the sole factory making iPods was causing a significant decrease in air quality affecting those in a 50-mile radius of the factory.
    - Would you be willing to pay an extra $50.00 to purchase an iPod knowing that the factory was using the additional funds to clean the air by making the factory "clean"?
        o If you lived 25 miles away?
        o If you lived 100 miles away?
        o If you lived 1,000 miles away?
        o What if the factory were in a foreign country?
        o Should it matter where the factory was located?

1.   Public Goods

"Public goods" are environmental benefits shared by everyone, but owned by no one.

Examples include:
- Air
- Scenic vistas
- Ecosystems

Ecosystems result from the interaction between living things and their environment.
- Living things include both flora (plant life) and fauna (animal life).

A healthy ecosystem provides services to the living things such as:
- Purifying air
- Purifying water
- Detoxifying and decomposing waste
- Renewing soil fertility
- Regulating climate
- Mitigating environmental calamities and phenomenon such as droughts and floods
- Controlling pests
- Pollinating plants

When even one ecosystem service fails and must be remedied, the cost of replacement is extremely high.
- Example: If nitrogen in the soil were depleted and had to be restored solely by fertilization, the lowest cost estimate for U.S. crops would be $45 billion and the cost for all land plants would approximate $320 billion.

Suggested Discussion Question and Activity
1. Is any one system more vital than any other system? Have the class debate this.
2. Break the class into groups and, after assigning a particular location (the Brazilian Rain Forest, the Mojave Desert, the African Serengeti, the Delaware Water Table, Michigan's Upper Peninsula, the Bering Sea, etc.), have the group choose one or two system services and report on the effects of its depletion or destruction in terms of:
   - Monetary costs
     - To repair or replenish
     - If repairing or replenishing is not done
   - Effects on flora and fauna within the system
   - Effects on other ecosystems

2.   *The Tragedy of the Commons*

The tragedy of the commons refers to the depletion of common resources without regard to future regeneration or replenishment.

The resources affected include both living resources and natural resources.

Suggested Discussion Questions and Activities
1. At what point does greed or striving for personal incentives affect the environment?
2. What is our responsibility with regard to preserving the environment for future generations? Our children? Our grandchildren?

3. Have the students do a critical analysis of their own resource use and examine whether they are, in fact, wastefully depleting a resource. (How long do they run the shower before getting in? Are their cars maintained so that air pollution is minimized? Would they ever consider carpooling or using public transportation?)

3. Collective Action and Free Riders

A collective action problem arises and worsens as the number of parties to the problem increases.
- There are increased negotiation costs.
- The more players involved, the more difficult it is to arrive at a consensus.

When one player adopts an environmentally-friendly stance, the likelihood that an abuser will take advantage of the situation increases. This abuser is called a free rider.

Suggested Discussion Questions
1. If one country seriously changes its practices in an environmentally-friendly way, does it make a real difference if other countries don't adopt similar policies? Have the class discuss the feasibility of worldwide change and enforcement.
2. Discuss what occurred when a situation as described in #1 above has occurred. (Example: The moratorium on whaling and Japan's refusal to acquiesce.)

4. Externalities

Externalities are costs to the general public that do not directly affect a company's bottom line.
- The cost of water pollution
- The cost of air pollution

Internalizing externalities will occur when the offending company is forced to account for the public damage caused to society.
- Regulation with the threat of fines or other penalties will force a company to internalize an externality.
- Providing a company with incentives to reduce a negative externality will also result in the internalization of the externality in a fruitful way.

Suggested Discussion Questions
1. Is internalizing externalities always a good thing for the environment? the consumer?
2. What are the ramifications of:
    - Regulations and fines to assure internalization of externalities?
    - Incentives to encourage internalization of externalities?

C.   *Mismatched Scales*

Natural boundaries and political boundaries are rarely identical.
- Environmental concerns are rarely, if even, considered when establishing political boundaries.
- Phenomena that affect the environment such as water and air pollution or wildlife concerns are not restricted to artificial political boundaries.
    - This is called geographic spillover.
        - Air pollution in the Midwest causes acid rain hundreds and thousands of miles away.
        - Water pollution causes wildlife concerns miles downstream from the pollution source.
        - Pollution in one country can have serious ramifications on other countries.

Transboundary problems pose significant challenges to collective action, both regarding national and international law problems.
- Agreement on uniform laws
- Monitoring compliance
- Enforcing penalties

Frequently, the rights and expectations between local and non-local citizens will be in direct conflict.

Environmental law implementation cannot be entirely reactive but must be proactive.
- Decisions and policies made today will prevent harm decades from today.
- Waiting until the problem has become critical means we have waited too long.

Suggested Discussion Questions and Activity
1. When, if ever, should the federal government have the right to dictate to a state how the state's land should be utilized?
2. When federally-owned land is located within a state's boundaries, when, if ever, should a state have the right to dictate how the federal land should be utilized?
3. Should uniform environmental laws be created alleviating the conflict of laws between states?
4. Should the local user of land have any rights to expectation of continued usage based on historical or prior family usage? Does it make sense to allow grandfathering in these cases?
5. Have the students research an extinct or endangered species and report:
    - What the root of the extinction or endangerment was or is.
    - Whether preventative measures enacted in a timely manner could have prevented the problem.
    - A cost comparison of the costs of early preventative measures weighed against the cost of reviving the endangered species or the cost to society or the environment of the extinction.

D.   Cognitive Biases

Everyone exhibits cognitive limitations and biases that affect our environmental views.
- A general failure to properly understand probability and statistics heightens the problem.
- Analyzing and accepting environmental tradeoffs requiring a cost-benefit analysis is also problematic for most people.
- The manner in which information is presented often slants the typical citizen's view.
    - 95% safe vs. 5% unsafe
    - People tend to overreact to unfamiliar risks based on the frequency of stories or articles reporting on the risk (called an *availability heuristic*).
    - *Availability heuristics* often lead to an *availability cascade* in which relatively small risks become widespread concerns with escalating importance to the general public.
    - Persistent *availability cascades* create an *anchoring effect,* making it extremely difficult to alter public perception.
- People tend to be overly optimistic with regard to the overcoming of environmental problems.
- A *self-enhancing attributional bias* leads people to be convinced that other people are to blame for environmental problems.
    - Factories, not drivers, cause or contribute to air pollution.
    - Farmers believe that they properly use water and the pollution and overuse of water is a city-caused problem.
- People often fail to accept their role in effecting environmental solutions.
    - People and nations suffer from *egocentric interpretations of fairness*.
        - "Other people should bear the burden, not me."
        - "I won't change until or unless everyone else changes."
        - All nations should share in the solution, not just the established highly industrial ones.

Suggested Discussion Questions and Activity
1. How many students believe that they contribute to environmental problems?
2. Discuss the point at which a personal inconvenience would cause students to ignore a potential solution.
3. The federal government has instituted incentives to reduce an individual's impact on the environment such as tax breaks for driving hybrid automobiles. Do the students agree with this policy?
4. If the classroom is Internet equipped, go to http://www.mec.ca/coop/communit/meccomm/ecofoot.htm and have one or more students take the quiz to determine their impact on the environment. If the classroom is not Internet equipped, have a number of students volunteer to take the quiz out of class and bring copies of their results in to share with the class. Follow with a discussion analyzing the results and perhaps making lifestyle suggestions that could positively impact the environment.

E.   Protected Interests

Who is actually protected by environmental legislation?
- The species protected by an endangered species act
- Researchers studying the endangered species are afforded protection to accomplish their work
- Future generations for whom the endangered species is preserved enjoys a benefit

Standing to sue becomes a very real issue because the animal or plant can't bring suit and all others are secondary or derivative plaintiffs.

Problems also arise when environmental protection groups are accused of caring more for animals than people when fighting development.

Suggested Discussion Question and Activity
1. Is it possible to measure the importance of animal and/or plant preservation in light of the wants and needs of human beings?
2. Have the students research the issue confronting the Tennessee Valley Authority when the Snail Darter was discovered during the planning of a dam project. Do they support the outcome? What if it was a species of alligator or a species of eagle rather than a two-inch fish thought to have been extinct?

II.   Four Analytical Frameworks

Criteria used for decision making must consider a number of variables.

Example: What should be considered when deciding whether to permit the use of a new pesticide?
- Potential harm to humans?
- Potential harm to animals?
- How the potential harm relates to potential benefits?

Four general frameworks are frequently utilized when faced with a sensitive decision:
- Focusing on ethical rights
    o Potential harms
- Addressing both environmental protection and development interests
    o Sustainable development
- Balancing risks through a utilitarian approach
    o Benefits to society in general
- Equitable distribution of cost and benefits amongst individuals and groups throughout society
    o Impact on minorities or underrepresented/less powerful people

Other considerations may include a pragmatic approach, incorporating parts of each of the four frameworks previously described.

A. *Environmental Rights*

Environmental law frequently takes the view that humans have the right to control the environment.

- In 1968 a constitutional amendment was proposed to recognize an "inalienable right to a decent environment."

Although defeated as an addition to the Constitution, environmental rights have been recognized through state constitutions and international treaties.

- 1972 Stockholm Declaration of the United Nations Conference on the Human Environment
    o "Common conviction" that people have:
        ▪ A "fundamental right to freedom, equality, and adequate conditions of life, in an environment of a quality that permits a life of dignity and wellbeing."
        ▪ A "solemn responsibility to protect and improve the environment for present and future generations."
- The Hawaiian constitution
    o Every person has "a right to a clean and healthful environment."
- Rights similar to the Hawaiian constitutional rights are contained in the Massachusetts, Montana, and Pennsylvania constitutions.

Judicial decisions and statutes frequently address environmental rights and the need for the protection of these rights.

- Stop H-3 Ass'n v. Dole, 870 F.2d 1419, 1430 (9th Cir.1989)
- The Clean Air Act
    o Requires ambient air standards "requisite to protect the human health"

Absolute protection from environmental hazards for all is unattainable because even the minutest levels of contamination may cause harm to some small segment of society.

- Only a zero pollution standard, an impossibility, would protect all.

Three prominent theories of "right" exist:

- Anthropocentric rights are rights pertaining to current and future generations of humans.
- Biocentric rights concern the rights of plants and animals other than humans.
- Ecocentric rights promote the protection of nature as a whole, frequently focusing on aesthetics.

Anthropocentric and biocentric rights frequently overlap.

- The Endangered Species Act was designed to protect human interests in the protection of plants and animals.

Suggested Discussion Questions and Activity
1. Can one be anthropocentric without being either biocentric and/or ecocentric?
2. Is it possible to adhere to one theory with no regard to the others?
3. Have the students identify an issue or situation in which each of the theories should take precedence over the others. Does the entire class agree? (Note that a failure to reach agreement highlights the challenge facing lawmakers.)

B.   *Sustainable Development*

Economic expansion is considered a key to ending poverty.

This goal of economic expansion and resultant growth of institutional infrastructure has resulted in the depletion of resources.

Development cannot be abandoned or even subordinated to environmental concerns; however, the two must be integrated.
- This integration is called sustainable development.

Sustainable development was defined at the 1992 Earth Summit in Rio de Janeiro as, "development that meets the needs of the present without compromising the ability of future generations to meet their own needs."
- Development and environmental protection are tied together.
- Intragenerational equity is recognized and sought.
- Growth is defined differently than development and the assumption that growth is good is put into perspective.
    - o Growth must be kept in perspective and within acceptable limits.

Suggested Discussion Question
1. Should newly emerging and developing countries be held to the same standards as highly developed established countries?
    - If yes, how can the country grow, compete with others economically, and solve poverty problems within its borders?
    - If no, how long, or at what point in its growth, should a country be permitted to violate "established" or "understood" standards before conformity becomes mandatory?

C.   *Utilitarianism and Cost-Benefit Analysis*

The government does a cost-benefit analysis when new laws or regulations are proposed.

Benefits anticipated are considered and weighed against possible costs.

Typical benefits and costs include:

Benefits	Costs
Avoided medical costs	Employment loss
Human lives saved	Reduced industrial production
Animal species saved	Reduced land development
Aesthetics	Costs of pollution control equipment
Anthropocentric concerns	Costs of enforcement

Economists would focus on pure monetary analysis, while the government cost-benefit analysis must be broader.
- Money is no doubt always a concern, it's just not the only concern.
- Where human life is a consideration, anthropocentric concerns may outweigh monetary considerations.
    o The EPA is forbidden from considering costs when setting national ambient air standards.
    o Costs may not be considered when promoting an act that jeopardizes the continued existence of an endangered species.

Decision making by lawmakers is difficult because groups are involved rather than individuals. Furthermore, the benefits afforded to a singular or small group often comes at the expense of a large group or groups.

Suggested Discussion Question
1. What do the students think? How about one billion dollars? One hundred million dollars? One million dollars? Does it matter how many people were helped? How should the cost relate to the amount of people helped?

D.   *Environmental Justice*

Environmental justice examines how the burdens of environmental harms and regulations are allocated amongst individuals and groups in society.
- Distributive issues gained prominence in 1978 when a proposal to dump tainted soil in Warren County, a poor region of North Carolina, was considered.
    o The proposed site was 64% African American and Native American.
    o Demonstrations were organized to stop the dumping.
        ▪ Although the demonstrations failed, the cause and issue became national news and showed a need for future consideration.

Following the Warren County demonstrations, research showed that minority communities bore a disproportionate share of environmental burdens. These burdens resulted in:
- Poor air quality
- Closer proximity to Superfund sites resulting in increased exposure to hazardous waste
- Increased incidences of lead poisoning
- Pesticide exposure

Claims are made that the placing of environmental hazards in or near minority areas is environmental racism.

Suggested Discussion Question
1. At what point does the powerful taking advantage of the less powerful become racism rather than politics?

PART I
Tools of the Trade

CHAPTER 3
The Practice of Environmental Protection

I.   Instrument Choice

Most Americans (80%) believe themselves to be environmentalists.

It is estimated by the EPA that only 2.5% of our GNP is allocated towards environmental protection issues.

Balancing the costs and efforts allocated towards social services, the military, the environment, and other pressing issues is a constant concern.
- The issues are many and the funds are limited.

Levels of protection are also subject to debate:
- How clean is clean?
- How safe is safe?
- What is important and what is not?
- What should be addressed first, second, third…etc.?

A.   *The Regulatory Toolkit*

See: *Madison v. Ducktown Sulphur, Copper & Iron Co.*, Supra

Courts find it difficult to address permanent damages.
- Past damages are usually simple to determine; however, future damages are speculative and often can't be accurately measured.
- Damages are frequently not caused by a single source.

Regulation addresses conduct and looks to the present and future rather than addressing the past.

Law focuses on injury and compensation while regulations address future conduct and prevention of future harm.
- Regulating conduct removes the need to analyze the reason or purpose of the conduct.
  - o Intent and/or negligence become secondary to results.

The common law is often described as reactive rather than proactive. Statutes and regulations, however, if properly researched and written, can address present and future conduct thus preventing harm.

A range of policy approaches is available to overcome the tragedy of the commons: the so-called "Five P's" of Prescriptive Regulation, Property Rights, Penalties, Payments, and Persuasion.

Suggested Discussion Activity
1. Explain (or remind) the students, what the role of courts in the legal and political process is. Issues to stress include standing, ripeness, and the separation of powers inherent in our system. The constitutional restriction against *ex post facto* laws should also be discussed.

1.   Prescriptive Regulation

Prescriptive regulation, also called command-and-control regulation, mandates how a resource is to be used in the future.

It occurs when limits are placed on the type of crops which may be planted, the number of animals that may be grazed, the amount of minerals that may be extracted from the ground, or the number of fish or other wildlife that may be caught or killed.

2.   Property Rights

Reliance on private property rights is a classic solution to the tragedy of the commons.
- Depleting your own property is much less desirable than depleting common property because:
  - o Blame can't be shifted to other
  - o Depletion directly affects the owner's property values
- Private property owners accept the concept of sustainability managed property because it is in their own best interests.

Technology, both simple and sophisticated, is necessary for private property rights to be protected. Examples include:
- Fences and barbed wire to keep other users out
- Fences and barbed wire to keep domestic farm stock in
- Scientific achievements to make property use more effective and profitable

Emphasizing private property rights facilitates the use of trading systems such as the use of credits.

Privatization of property does have potential problems.
- If a commons area were divided and granted or sold to individuals:
  - o Who should get it?
  - o Can it be distributed fairly?

- o How could costs be allocated?
- o Owners could abandon environmentally safe or friendly uses when faced with the opportunity for economic benefit or windfall

a.   Tradable Permits

A variant of creating property rights is the use of tradable permits.
- Property rights are created in the form of marketable use, emissions, or extractions rights.
- The government can set a predetermined level of harmful activity that it will permit and can regulate the activity with some entities below the limit and some above.
  - o Limits and protections are therefore monitored without market influence.

Suggested Discussion Questions

In theory, when permits are used to regulate use, those who consider the use to be most valuable will pay extra to obtain permits.
1. How can the regulating body create fairness in the allocation or resale of permits to protect the less wealthy from the more affluent?
2. Should such protections even exist, or should the market system simply police itself?

3.   Financial Penalties

The most direct way to internalize externalities is through charges, taxes, or liability.
- In theory, environmentally harmful activities should be charged the cost of the harm imposed.
- Two practical obstacles:
  - o Getting the price right
  - o Passing environmental taxes

4.   Financial Payments

Governments can discourage certain polluting activities through penalties but, equally, can encourage beneficial activities through subsidizing them.

While government payments for environmentally-friendly activities have great potential, most government payments have negative environmental impacts.
- In addition to internalizing the environmental costs that are now outside the market, getting the price right so that resources can be allocated efficiently also requires the elimination of price distortions, which typically occur in the form of government subsidies.

5.   Persuasion

Information production and dissemination is considered a softer approach to regulation than utilizing prescriptive regulation and market approaches.

Reflexive laws require people to keep a record of their activities with the record subsequently published.
- Harms or abuses are therefore publicized.
- Education can be formulated to combat future harms or abuses.

B.   Putting the Toolkit to Work

Effective regulation frequently utilizes a combination of regulatory methods. This combination varies based on the circumstance being addressed.

For example, if addressing the regulation of a proposed greenhouse gas law:
- The common law would not be effective because causation could not be established easily.
- Prescriptive regulation would prove practical; however, the reliance on a strict standard technical approach does not encourage industry to exceed standards once they are met.
- Financial penalties seem workable. Emission fees could be levies based on the amount of greenhouse gases emitted; tax credits or tax deductions might also be effective.
- Via property rights, the establishment of a trading market may increase efficiency; typical cap-and-trade programs establish emission levels, allocate emissions among sources, and issue permits to sources that allow each to emit a given quantity of that pollutant.

Information disclosure will make the issue publicly known and having to publicize one's actions may cause pressure to act more for the public good. Consumers can also then put pressure on companies by purchasing from environmentally-friendly companies to the detriment of abusers.

Suggested Discussion Questions
1. Have any of the students ever balanced a purchasing decision on a political issue?
2. Would the students pay more for a product if it was produced by an environmentally-friendly company? If so, how much more?

C.   Instrument Design Issues

Agreeing on the proper instruments to use for environmental regulation is a persistently debatable issue.
- Each regulatory instrument has both its positives and negatives.

- Three issues must be addressed: the debate over relative efficiency, the relevance of administrative costs, and the choice of regulatory target.

Critics of so-called "inefficient" prescriptive regulations contend there should be a greater reliance on market instruments.
- However, many market instruments (e.g., tradable permits) necessarily rely on prescriptive regulation.

The classic response to those concerned with administrative costs is that, while a health-based standard is often attractive, economical, and certainly can be effective, pollution and harm may continue even when the health of those in proximity to the problem seems to be safe.
- For example, the factory spewing pollutants that blow in the wind over the ocean rather than towards the surrounding community may cause problems hundreds or thousands of miles away, but not in the factory's community.
- Health-based standards and technology-based standards are often at odds and reaching a compromise is often difficult.

The choice of a regulatory target and goal is as important as choosing the instrument to apply.
- Who should be regulated?
- What should be regulated?

The government cannot regulate everything nor can it regulate everyone. Choosing the best targets allows for more effective regulation.

Suggested Discussion Question
1. Using the book's pesticide example, discuss the effects of pesticide regulation on the following:
   - Research and development laboratories in industry
   - Universities and colleges with agriculture schools or departments
   - Distributors
   - Retailers
   - Commercial users/purchasers such as farmers
   - Commercial users/purchasers such as Parks Departments in cities and towns
   - Residential users/purchasers
   - Citizens/taxpayers in general

D.   Where to Go From Here?

Environmental protection is a very young field, existing just over 40 years.

This new status makes environmental protection:
- Dynamic
- Constantly changing
- Often criticized

Criticisms stem from its perceived inefficiency.
- Legal requirements are frequently very rigid.
- Rules are often too restrictive.
- Enforcement can result in higher costs than necessary.
- The need for protections is often questioned.

The 1990 EPA Scientific Advisory Board's report on "Reducing Risk" found little correlation between EPA budget priorities and scientists' risk rankings.
- As a result, many have called for stronger reliance on cost-benefit analysis and risk assessment.

The laws themselves create inefficiency because of their crisis management tenor.
- The reactive nature of enactment is very often spurred by news articles and post-catastrophe response rather than proactive protection.
- Environmental laws also tend to be very complex and sometimes ambiguous.
  - With over 11,000 pages of federal environmental law, overlap and conflicting requirements make compliance and enforcement difficult.
  - State and local laws only add to the difficulty.

With this unsettled yet vibrant area, unintended consequences are unavoidable.
- Examples:
  - When hazardous waste burial was curtailed, the land quality revived; however, the burning of the waste increased air pollutant levels.
  - Superfund initiatives creating liability and discouraging "brownfield sites" resulted in the movement of industry toward "greenfield sites," exasperating the problem of urban sprawl.

Fairness in implementation and enforcement continues to be a problem particularly when determining who was the cause and who should shoulder blame.

The aforementioned problems have resulted in a constant reinvention of programs and projects as problems arise and changes become necessary.

Suggested Discussion Questions
1. Is it always necessary for there to be an equilibrium between costs and risks?
2. Would the utilization of a required cost-benefit analysis result in the quantifying of life—plant, animal, and human? If so, who makes the decisions?

II. The Administration of Environmental Protection

To understand the practice of environmental law one must first grasp the broader legal framework within which it operates.

Administrative law sets the parameters for how agencies may implement these statutes and constitutional law sets the limits of governmental authority.

A. Basics of Administrative Law

Administrative law makes the government more open, responsive, and accountable to the public.
- It concerns how agencies operate.
- It helps to preserve the government's separation of powers.

Administrative law is important to environmental law and protection because environmental law and protection is regulated through administrative agencies.

Administrative departments were first established in 1789 with the creation of the Departments of State, Treasury, and War. The number has grown such that the current alphabetical list of agencies encompasses over nine pages in *fine print*.

Environmental related agencies generally fall into two models:
- Those with scientific expertise
- Those with a focus on interest group representation
  - Agency capture occurs when an agency aligns itself with the industry they were established to regulate.

Agency capture must be guarded against. This occurs when agencies so closely align themselves with the industries they're supposed to regulate that the public interest is lost in the process.

Agency self-interest is another problem that must be monitored. This occurs when an agency allows politics to influence its decision making.

The governing law to which administrative agencies fall under is the Administrative Procedures Act (APA).
- Sets procedures for promulgating rules
- Sets rules for adjudication conflicts
- Determines guidelines for judicial review

Suggested Discussion Questions
1. Since an agency's budget is often controlled by either the President or by Congress, and the actual continued existence of the agency itself can be determined by Congress, can administrative agencies ever be truly autonomous?

2. Discuss the difference between executive agencies and independent agencies. How does the President's removal power regarding the heads of executive agencies possibly affect an agency's operations?

1.   Rulemaking

The APA breaks most agency actions into the categories of rulemaking and adjudication.

Administrative rules are frequently a result of delegation resulting from statutory authority.
- Statutes are passed with the agency designated to do "gap filling" to make the statute meaningful and complete.

Environmental rule creation falls under the category of informal rulemaking.
- Notice of proposed rules is published.
- Comments are solicited from the public.
- No formal hearing with cross examination of witnesses is held.
- The final rule is published in the Federal Register.

Informal rulemaking may not be arbitrary and capricious.
- Responses to the categories of public comments must also be published establishing a justification for the rule.
- Under judicial review, courts are not permitted to add procedural requirements to rules promulgated with inadequate procedural protections.
- Courts are also limited in their interpretation of the language within rules and must defer to the agency.

The approach to statutory interpretation that the U.S. Supreme Court adopted in *Chevron U.S.A., Inc. v. Natural Resources Defense Council* (the so-called "*Chevron* two-step") asks two questions.
- Has Congress spoken directly to the precise question at issue?
  - If so, then the court must determine whether the agency action conforms to the unambiguous Congressional mandate.
- Has Congress *not* directly addressed the specific question (or addressed it ambiguously)?
  - If not, the court must decide only whether the agency's answer is based on a "permissible" construction of the statute.

Suggested Discussion Questions
1. Should courts have the right to fix procedural problems related to administrative rules? Why or why not?
2. Should a court be limited when interpreting language contained in a rule? Does the "plain meaning rule" work when scientific language is prevalent or when new terminology is being created by the rule itself?

2. Adjudication

A key to proper adjudication is adhering to proper procedural processes.

Proper procedural processes must be in accord with APA requirements, special rules published in the Federal Register, as well as Constitutional requirements contained in the 5th and 14th amendments.

3. Final Agency Action

Agencies take many actions that are neither rulemaking nor adjudication.

Administrative law prevents challenges to agency actions in court until the doctrines of finality (i.e., the action has been decided within the agency), ripeness (the issue is ready for judicial resolution) and exhaustion (the challenging party's opportunities for review within the agency process are exhausted).

When agency actions can be challenged in court, judges must "compel agency action unlawfully withheld or unreasonably delayed" as well as "hold unlawful" actions found to be "arbitrary, capricious, an abuse of discretion, or otherwise not in accordance with law."

III. Constitutional Issues in Environmental Policy

Regardless of any rules, statutes, or other laws promulgated, the U.S. Constitution remains as the supreme law of the land.
- The supremacy clause established the preemption of state law when in conflict with federal law.
- The "dormant commerce clause" restricts the states' authority to ban the importation of hazardous waste into the state.

Suggested Discussion Questions
1. Since environmental protections are such a new and relatively unsettled area of the law, is it too soon to use constitutional amendments as a tool to ensure public good?
2. When the Constitution was written over 200 years ago, there was no thought given to the environment. Were the Constitution to be written today, would or should recognition for environmental protections be included?

A. Congressional Powers

Congressional action in environmental protection has stemmed primarily from its commerce power.

The use of the commerce power is, however, limited.

In *United States v. Lopez*, the U.S. Supreme Court ruled on the attempt of Congress to regulate gun possession near schools using its commerce power. The Court decided that commerce power relates only to:

- The use of the channels of interstate commerce
- Activities that threaten the avenues of interstate commerce
- Activities having a substantial effect on interstate commerce
  - Mere impact on interstate commerce is not enough to support Congressional regulation.

Pollution and regulation of hazardous substance laws do present a broad and substantial enough impact to allow for Congressional regulation.

Regulation of local land uses is not firmly within *Lopez* interpretation guidelines and is easier to challenge.

- Land use decisions have traditionally been under local government authority.
- The connection between local regulations and interstate commerce is not always easy to establish.

Although all challenges to federal regulation of local land use have failed, the federal regulations have often been interpreted to avoid the constitution al issue.

B. *Legislative Delegation*

Congress itself lacks the expertise to make informed technical and scientific decisions.

To facilitate the proper oversight and promulgation of rules, Congress establishes and delegates these duties to administrative agencies. Using their expertise, agencies:

- Provide definitions of terms
- Establish acceptable and reasonable standards
- Guide future policy

Congress has the duty to determine policy and when this obligation is, or appears to be, delegated to an administrative body, questions arise as to the propriety of the delegation. This is a fine line that is sometimes blurred for the sake of efficiency and results.

Suggested Discussion Question and Activity

1. Discuss the necessity of delegation in this context as well as a general business context. Do the students agree that delegation is necessary for business and government to operate?
2. Have the students research an agency's "charge" and determine the types of powers that have been delegated to the agency. Do any of these delegations fall into a possible policy making area?

C.   Regulatory Takings

The Constitution allows for the taking of privately-owned property for the public use or good:
- When just compensation is paid
- When the taking is indeed for the public use or good

Courts must frequently determine whether an administrative regulation becomes a taking.
- Is the value of private property diminished if an endangered species living on the property limits the use or development of the property?
- When the burial of hazardous waste was banned and burning the waste ensued, did the reduced air quality in surrounding areas affect land value?
- Generally, is the devaluation of property actually a taking when ownership remains unchanged?

Suggested Discussion Questions
1. Is devaluation of property value a taking?
2. Is the modern definition consistent with what the writers of the Constitution intended?

The Supreme Court, in *Penn Central Transportation Co. v. New York City,* determined that no set formula existed and that decisions regarding regulatory takings should be made on an ad hoc basis. Their test examined:
- The extent of interference with distinct investment-backed expectations
- The nature of such interference
- The purposes of the governmental regulation

Compensation for regulatory takings has been upheld:
- When the rights of an owner to exclude others from private property have been interfered with
- When there has been a permanent physical occupation of private property by the public
- When a landowner has been deprived of *all* economically viable use of private property (*Lucas v. South Carolina Costal Council*)

Several arguments for compensation have been formulated by affected landowners:
- If people may be prohibited from entering private land, endangered species protections permit the entrance of that species onto the land causing devaluation.
  - Rejected – A native species of wildlife is not the equivalent of human occupation of the land
- Land should be able to be parceled for application of *Lucas* so that if a portion of land loses all economic viability there should be compensation for that specific portion.
  - This denominator question has been rejected because the landowner continues to enjoy economic use of the remaining property.

o In *Tahoe-Sierra Preservation Council v. Tahoe Regional Planning Agency*, the court reaffirmed the parcel as a whole approach and upheld *Lucas*.

Suggested Discussion Question
1. Do the students agree with the decision in *Palozzolo v. Rhode Island* allowing a landowner who purchased property subject to a published regulation affecting land use to bring suit challenging the publicly known and established regulation?

IV. How Citizen Groups Shape Environmental Law

Those familiar with environmental issues credit the existence of a dynamic and forceful movement as the prime driver of environmental regulation.
- The Audubon Society (now the National Audubon Society) started in 1886 with approximately 40,000 members.
- The Sierra Club, Izaak Walton League, and Wilderness Society soon followed.
- By 1960, over 300,000 Americans had memberships in major conservation organizations.
- The first Earth Day in 1970 was followed with even further increased interest and participation.

A. *Lobbying for Legislative and Administrative Action*

Environmental groups raise money from the general public needed to combat the deep pocket resources of industry.

Although a segment of the public continues to be free riders, environmental groups have been able to raise money; because their entire focus is narrowly defined in environmental issues, lobbying efforts have been relatively successful.

The Clean Water Act and the Clean Air Act are two examples of legislation directly influenced through the efforts of environmental organizations.

B. *Citizen Suits*

Every major federal environmental law passed since 1970 has included a citizen suit provision except the Federal Insecticide, Fungicide, and Rodenticide Act.
- Note that the FIFRA was promulgated by an agricultural rather than an environmental committee.

Citizen suit provisions allow:
- Filing suit against anyone, public or private, alleged to be in violation of an environmental law
- Individuals or groups to sue the EPA administrator or other governmental officials who fail to enforce non-discretionary Congressional obligations

Statutes frequently limit the type of violation that may be prosecuted by citizen suits.

Citizens, in effect, act as private prosecutors enforcing the law.
- Remedies are primarily limited to injunctive relief.
- Monetary damages, when authorized, are paid to the U.S. government and not to the "prosecutor."

In *Gwaltney of Smithfield, Ltd. v. Chesapeake Bay Foundation*, the court limited citizen suits to continuing or intermittent violations, precluding suits for past violations.

Citizen suits may not be filed where the federal or a state government has already commenced suit or is diligently pursuing prosecution.

Defendants must reimburse citizens who prevail in citizen suits for costs including reasonable attorney fees.
- The court calculates the fee by multiplying the reasonable time spent on the suit by the attorney's private representation fees to calculate the "lodestar" amount due.

C.   Standing

Standing to bring a lawsuit generally involves four components:
- The plaintiff has suffered injury
- The injury resulted from the defendant's action
- The court has the power to provide appropriate relief
- The injury must be within the zone of interests that the law is supposed to protect

Citizen suits will fail when the standing requirement cannot be met.

Groups alleging standing must show that a member or members have suffered injury. In *Sierra Club v. Morton*, the court maintained that injury need not be physical but may include aesthetic or recreational injury.

After *Sierra Club v. Morton*, the Supreme Court seemed to be very amenable to finding standing in environmentally-related suits. This began to change in the mid-1990s, when the Court showed a new willingness to interpret standing claims more narrowly.

In *Lujan v. Defenders of Wildlife*, the Court would not grant standing to sue based on U.S. agency actions overseas regarding endangered species.
- Affidavits were filed stating that members had traveled to affected areas and enjoyed an endangered species and would be deprived of that enjoyment were they to return.
- The court found this argument lacking.
  - Actual or imminent injury was required rather that speculative potential injury.

- o Mere professional or personal interest in studying the species was similarly insufficient.
- Importantly, the Court decided that "Congress has the power to define injuries and articulate chains of causation" that otherwise would not provide standing, when promulgating a law.

The ability of the Court to provide adequate or appropriate remedies for injuries is a constant problem when bringing environmental suits.
- This is the basis for precluding citizen suits based on past violations.

Determining the appropriateness of a plaintiff with regard to being in a statute or rules zone of interest is a significant issue.

Courts must weigh the protections provided in the suit against economic interests of the plaintiff to truly assess the purpose of the suit.
- Nevertheless, citizen suits may be brought by anyone showing injury.
- Issues regarding the purpose of the suit are not a standing-related issue but a matter for the court to decide at trial. (see: *Bennett v. Spear*)

Lawsuits brought to address climate change have raised new and unique standard issues because of the difficulty of linking specific damage to climate change, the similar harm suffered by widespread parties, and the challenge of remedying climate change through any single action or policy (see: *Massachusetts v. Environmental Protection Agency)*,

Suggested Discussion Question and Activity
1. Can the students identify an environmentally sensitive issue that they could personally establish standing to bring suit?
2. Have the students prepare a complaint as plaintiff-related to the issue raised.

PART II
Pollution Law

CHAPTER 4
The Clean Air Act

I.   The Challenges of Regulating Air Pollution

The Clean Air Act Amendments of 1970 (CAA) are the nation's pre-eminent environmental laws.
- The CAA created uniform, national standards.
- The CAA reflected the age's technological optimism as well as dissatisfaction with poor urban air quality.

The CAA was intended to solve America's air pollution problems within ten years.
- Today, our air is cleaner than at the time of the CAA's passage.
- However, many of America's largest cities still do not meet the CAA's clean air requirements.

One cannot understand the CAA's structure without first grasping the air pollution problem.
- By itself, air pollution rarely kills people; it mainly aggravates health problems such as bronchitis, pneumonia, and asthma.
- In urban areas, chief health concerns revolve around breathing smog (O_3)
  - According to the American Lung Association, lung disease kills over 400,000 Americans annually.
  - More than 35 million Americans suffer from chronic lung disease.
  - The death rate for lung disease has remained steady over the past several years while the other leading causes of death have dramatically decreased.
- Other pollutants such as nitrogen oxide (NO_x) and sulfur dioxide (SO_2) create acid rain.
  - In addition to exacerbating our health problems, acid rain can damage forests and aquatic ecosystems.

Air pollution is difficult to regulate because pollutants arise from many different sources.
- Vehicle emissions account for over half of total CO emissions, almost half of NOx, and more than 25 percent of volatile organic compounds (VOCs).
- Power plants are important emitters of SO_2 and NO_x.
- Incinerators and factories are major sources of hazardous air pollutants.
- All of these pollutants merge in the atmosphere, crossing county and state lines—so which jurisdiction is responsible for regulation?

Drafters of CAA needed to create a truly national law covering an entire class of pollutants from a wide variety of sources. The four main policy questions the CAA needed to address were:

- What to regulate: Which pollutants should be regulated, and should some take priority over others?
- How much to regulate: What level of protection from air pollution is required?
- Where to regulate: Regulate at the source of the pollution, or where people live and are affected by it?
- How to regulate: Should all polluters be treated the same? Why or why not?

A.   *National Ambient Air Quality Standards (NAAQS)*

See: *Lead Industries Association v. EPA*, Supra

The basis of the CAA is its treatment of the most common pollutants in the outside air—called *criteria pollutants*.

- Criteria pollutants—such as O_3, NO_x, CO, and SO_2—are emitted from numerous or diverse sources and can endanger public health or welfare.
- The CAA requires criteria pollutants not to exceed uniform levels at *any* outside areas accessible to the general public.

National Ambient Air Quality Standards (NAAQS) are set for each criteria pollutant at a level that must "protect the public health" with an "adequate margin of safety."

- In *Lead Industries Association v. EPA*, courts ruled that EPA can determine appropriate margin of safety.
- NAAQS levels must be based only on health considerations, not economic or technical feasibility.

There are two types of NAAQS:

- Primary standards protect human health.
- Secondary standards protect the public welfare (e.g., animals, wildlife, water, etc.).

NAAQS apply uniformly to all regions of the nation.

- The uniform approach, along with EPA's prohibition to consider costs and benefits, have been criticized as inefficient.
  - o Health impacts of dirty air vary from place to place, as do control costs.
  - o Individuals living in rural areas may be "overprotected" from danger.
- The uniform approach is easier to administer than more flexible local standards, which might be subject to local political pressure.
- Our growing understanding of air pollution's health effects blunts accusations of "overprotection."
- A uniform national law prevents states from becoming "pollution havens," accepting lower environmental standards in exchange for industry and jobs.

Suggested Discussion Questions

1. What suggestions do you have for further controlling air pollution? How would those ideas be enforced? Who would have responsibility for enforcing them?
2. How severe is the level of air pollution in your community? What are its effects? What are some measures your community has taken to protect itself from air pollution? Is your community "overprotected" from the dangers?

1.   State Implementation Plans (SIPs)

Implementation of the uniform approach of the NAAQS is somewhat tempered.

- EPA sets national ambient air quality standards; states regulate emissions so as to meet EPA standards.
- Each state must submit a State Implementation Plan (SIP) explaining how it will achieve the NAAQS.

In practice, however, exceptions in the CAA return much regulatory control to the federal government. (Example: New Source Performance Standards.)

- Main activity for states involves tightening standards on *existing* sources.
- EPA looks only at whether states will meet the NAAQS; it does not examine all state issues in detail. This gives states great latitude in how they regulate existing sources.

If EPA believes a SIP will not meet the NAAQS, it may establish a Federal Implementation Plan (FIP) that supersedes the SIP.

- EPA's limited authority and money has muted the threat of issuing FIPs to states.

Non-attainment of NAAQS standards has been the most challenging aspect of the CAA's history; forcing compliance has been extremely difficult.

- Southern California has long been notorious for non-attainment.
- EPA has been ineffective in dealing with non-attainment.
    o Threat of a FIP is rarely used.
    o EPA could deny federal highway or sewage treatment funds.
- Originally, states were to meet NAAQS by 1975; deadlines have been changed repeatedly. This is unsurprising, given the enormous costs and efforts involved for some areas to meet the standards.
    o Example: In 1988, EPA concluded that most traffic and major business activity in Southern California would need to be prohibited in order to bring Los Angeles into attainment.

The 1990 Clean Air Act Amendments broke down attainment goals into achievable, intermediate steps.

- Non-attainment areas are now divided into five categories—marginal, moderate, serious, severe, extreme. States no longer need to meet NAAQS in their entirety, all at once.

Suggested Discussion Question and Activity
1. What legislation does your state have in place to control pollution?
2. Have students do library or Internet research to determine which states are the most polluted. What are those states doing to control pollution? Are those controls helping? Divide the students in groups, and have each group report on one of the states with the highest pollution rates.

B.   New Source Performance Standards (NSPS) and Grandfathered Sources

CAA regulates air pollution both at the source and at the point of impact.
- The SIP process allows states to regulate emissions from existing stationary sources such as incinerators, power plants, and factories.
- EPA sets standards—called New Source Performance Standards (NSPS)—for pollutants from new or modified stationary sources.

The NSPS provision assumes that new and existing stationary sources will be treated differently.
- High standards for new facilities promote technological development. But this would also apply if older facilities were covered.
- Political reasons: Exempting existing sources eased passage of the CAA in 1970.
- "Grandfathered" plants do not need to meet NSPS requirements unless they undertake major modifications.
  - o Grandfathering allows older power plants to emit 4 to 10 times more SO_2 and NO_x per megawatt-hour than new sources, thus shifting some costs of control onto future businesses.
- The plan was that grandfathered plants would shut down eventually over time, making way for newer facilities that needed to comply with NSPS provisions.
  - o But does grandfathering create an incentive to continue operating older facilities for as long as possible?
  - o EPA has alleged this is exactly what a number of utilities have done over the past 30 years.

Why should federal government be responsible for regulating major new sources?
- Federal regulation is more efficient.
- Federal regulation reduces the impact that influential local industries might have over local standards.
- National standards prevent states from becoming "pollution havens."

Suggested Discussion Questions
1. Does grandfathering create an incentive to continue operating older industrial facilities for as long as possible? Explain your answer.
2. Do you agree that the federal government should be responsible for regulating major new sources of pollution? Why or why not?

C. Mobile Sources and Technology-Forcing

Mobile sources (cars, trucks, buses) are major air polluters, responsible for most non-compliance with ozone and CO standards.

The CAA regulates mobile sources of air pollution.
- Title I: Cleaner fuel mandated for some areas; improved vapor recovery systems at the gas pump.
- Title II: Tailpipe emission standards.
- Since the CAA, lead in the air has decreased by over 90 percent, though more vehicles are on the road now than in 1970.
- The main reason for federal, rather than state, authority over mobile source standards seems to have been the auto industry, which would have been severely crippled had it been required to manufacture different cars for different state standards.

The 1970 CAA required a 90 percent reduction of VOCs and CO emissions in car exhaust by 1975, and a 90 percent reduction of NO_x by 1976—a classic example of "technology-forcing."
- Why such tough standards, when technology to achieve these standards did not exist at the time?
  - Technological optimism
  - Public cynicism toward automakers, who had just been found guilty of conspiring to suppress emission control technology
  - Congress's judgment of what was needed to protect public health
- Technology-forcing provides a powerful way to achieve quick, dramatic results, but also requires strong political support to ensure a credible threat if goals are not met.
- Technology-forcing can also sometimes force the wrong technology. Example: Electric cars, which were costly to develop and were unsuccessful in the marketplace.

Regulation of mobile sources demonstrates that there are usually multiple ways to solve pollution problems, and that tradeoffs are inevitable.
- Example: The least expensive way for automakers to improve fuel efficiency is to make vehicles lighter, but this makes them more dangerous in the event of a crash.

Suggested Discussion Activities
1. Poll the class to determine how many students would consider purchasing a hybrid car. What are the reasons some students would purchase one? What are the reasons some students wouldn't consider one?
2. Have students write a short paper on hybrid cars, answering such questions as: What is the average cost of a hybrid? What are the cost savings over the life of the car? How do hybrids affect pollution? Is the cost of a hybrid worth the benefits? Where are most hybrids sold? Are sales projected to rise in the future?

D.   Trading

The desire to reduce air pollution has provided many opportunities for experimentation and fine-tuning of the CAA's regulatory approaches—most obviously in the area of trading.
- Two key challenges to CAA: (1) cleaning the air while (2) allowing economic growth and resultant pollution. Trading mechanisms help achieve this.

Bubbling is the simplest form of trading.
- Draw an imaginary bubble over your industrial site and regulate only the total emissions from the bubble, rather than emissions from each individual smokestack.

Netting is similar to bubbling.
- Facilities increase emissions in one source but reduce a similar amount of emissions from another on-site source.

Offsets occur within a non-attainment area; they rely on both bubbling and the trading of pollution rights. A new source may not pollute unless it offsets emissions by reductions from other area sources.
- 1990 CAA amendments built on use of offsets by requiring stronger offset ratios depending on the level of non-attainment.
- Offsets sometimes create problems when plants try to sell them to a new source.

Separate facilities can also trade rights to pollute.
- Government decides how much total pollution to allow, then allocates pollution allowances among the regulated facilities.

CAA's first use of trading involved reducing lead in gasoline. Lead content credits were allocated among refiners, who could trade them among one another or bank them for future use.

CAA's treatment of acid rain has created the most comprehensive trading program in the world.
- History of dealing with acid rain problem pits "dirty coal" Appalachian states, injured upwind states, and "clean coal" Western states against one another.
- Initial regulation of Midwestern power plants using "dirty" coal resulted in their building taller smokestacks, dispersing acid rain even more.
- Next cheapest way to cut sulfur emissions would be to burn "clean" coal, but this would economically damage local Appalachian communities.
- Compromise: In 1977, CAA required all new utilities to use "scrubbers" to remove sulfur from smokestack emissions.
  - This seemed overprotective for many plants already using low-sulfur coal.
- In 1990, new CAA amendments repealed scrubber requirement and instituted performance-based standards and tradable emissions allowances. There are three sorts of allowances:

o   Allowances are allocated by the CAA to existing plants. Bonus allowances are given to plants using "clean coal" or other appropriate technology.
o   Plants that need additional allowances can buy them from other plants.
o   EPA holds auctions for new allowances.

In theory, trading is better than source-specific regulation because it increases efficiencies.
- As long as you are using control technology at your facility to satisfy standards, there is no incentive to reduce emissions further.
- Under the trading system, reduced emissions can be sold on the market to sources that find it expensive to reduce their own emissions. This makes it worth a plant's while to reduce emissions.

But trading also has its drawbacks.
- Property rights must be secure and costs (to identify buyers and sellers as well as transaction costs of doing the deal) must be low or few trades will occur.
- Trading can lead to hot spots—areas of pollution concentration—and environmental justice concerns. (Example: Old Vehicle Scrapping Program in Los Angeles, which resulted in a hot spot near two Latino communities.)

A 2008 decision from the D.C. Circuit Court of Appeals (*North Carolina v. EPA*) has placed the future of some trading programs in doubt.
- The case challenged EPA's proposed Clean Air Interstate Rule (CAIR), which was designed to address the regional problem of NO_x and SO_2 emissions.
- Under CAIR, states could create their own SIPs for these pollutants or join a more cost-effective regional cap and trade program.
- However, the CAA "prohibits sources 'within the state' from 'contribut[ing] significantly to nonattainment in . . . any other state . . .'" The court held that CAIR could violate this requirement.

Suggested Discussion Activity
1. Divide the class into two groups and have them debate the pros and cons of "dirty coal" versus "clean coal." Have one group represent the "dirty coal" Appalachian states and the other group represent the "clean coal" Western states.

E.   *Prevention of Significant Deterioration (PSD)*

New major air pollution sources must employ NSPS as well as engage in trading if they are in non-attainment areas.
- However, CAA's Prevention of Significant Deterioration (PSD) requirements do not necessarily make it feasible for a company to build a new plant in a region already in attainment.
- New major sources in PSD areas must use "the best available control technologies," which are usually stricter than the NSPS.

The PSD program divides the country into three classes of areas with different levels of restriction.

- Class I areas include national parks; Class II areas cover most of the rest of the country; there are no Class III areas.
- A region's class category determines the amount of development allowed through "increments," which place an upper limit on the increase in ambient concentration of air pollutants.

The PSD program is puzzling, since NAAQS are met and there are no resultant health issues. Possible explanations:

- Desire to preserve clean air in undeveloped areas and national parks.
- Program limits industry movement from dirty to clean areas and ensures that non-attainment areas can still draw new businesses by making it expensive to move into PSD areas.

F.   Air Toxics

In 1999, EPA reported emissions of over 10 billion pounds of hazardous air pollutants (HAPs)—airborne chemicals that harm human health or the environment.

Section 112 of the CAA of 1970 required EPA to regulate HAPs by compiling a list of covered pollutants and setting National Emission Standards for Hazardous Air Pollutants (NESHAPs).

- Program aimed to provide "an ample margin of safety to protect the public health."
- But the program's progress was slow:
  - o What was an ample margin of safety? This was unknown for many HAPs.
  - o Would health and environmental benefits of zero emissions for certain HAPs be worth the economic cost?

NRDC v EPA ("vinyl chloride" case) addressed how EPA should determine ample margin of safety for HAPs:

- EPA must first determine a safe level based on scientific data, not considering cost or technological feasibility.
  - o "Safe" is not same as "risk-free." Zero risk was not the goal.
- After determining safety levels, EPA could take into account costs and technological feasibility to set a standard stricter than that dictated purely by safety concerns.

Because of slow progress of the NESHAPs program, 1990 CAA Amendments revamped air toxin regulation.

- Section 112 was changed from a purely health-based risk assessment to a hybrid process, and 189 different HAPs are regulated.
- New and major sources must meet emission levels determined by the Maximum Achievable Control Technology (MACT).

- MACT has issued standards for far more HAPs than under NESHAP, because it is easier to determine achievable control technologies for specific HAPs than to set emission levels at an ample margin to protect the public health.

G.   The CAA of Tomorrow

CAA has evolved considerably since its inception, and will undoubtedly continue to do so.

Ultimately, stricter regulation may be less effective than changes in lifestyle and personal habits, such as using mass transit rather than personal automobiles.

Next chapter of the CAA is already being written—whether and how to apply the law to greenhouse gases, which pose dramatically different challenges than criteria or hazardous air pollutants.

Suggested Discussion Questions
1. Where do you see the Clean Air Act evolving in the next 10 years? 25 years? 100 years? Will the CAA play a role in climate change?
2. Does your community offer mass transit? If so, do many people use it? What incentives could be offered to encourage more people to use mass transit, both in your community and in other cities?

PART II
Pollution Law

CHAPTER 5
Global Air Pollution

I.   Ozone Depletion

By 2009, 195 nations had ratified the Montreal Protocol to address ozone depletion. The framers of the Protocol faced a number of difficulties:
- Scientific uncertainty about the scale of depletion
- Divided international community
- Potentially high transaction costs
- The difficult global nature of the problem

Ozone depletion presents problems unlike traditional air and water pollution, since it is a global problem rather than a more localized national or regional problem. The Montreal Protocol was the first treaty to address the global character of a set of pollutants.

A.   The Science of Ozone Depletion

Ozone (O_3) is a simple molecule of three oxygen atoms; it occurs naturally in the atmosphere.
- It is most highly concentrated in the middle of the stratosphere (the "ozone layer"), where it protects the earth by absorbing harmful UV-B radiation from the sun.

Chlorofluorocarbons (CFCs) were developed in the 1920s by General Motors as a substitute for ammonia and sulfur dioxide refrigerants.
- By the early 1970s, the role of CFCs in the destruction of ozone was known; but 1974 research by Rowland and Molina first explained their potential role in the destruction of the ozone layer.
  o As CFCs rise into the stratosphere, ultraviolet radiation would destroy them, releasing chlorine and chlorine oxide molecules, which would in turn set off a chain-reaction destroying thousands of ozone molecules.
  o CFCs acted as a catalyst, ultimately reducing the concentration of ozone in the stratosphere and therefore its ability to absorb radiation.

Increased UV-B radiation has serious consequences on earth:
- Impacts on human health: skin cancers, cataracts, sunburns, suppressed immune systems
- Reduced agricultural yields
- Reduced growth of marine phytoplankton, the base of the ocean food chain
- Damage to midge larvae, the base of many fresh-water ecosystems

Suggested Discussion Question and Activity
1. Has ozone depletion personally affected your community or its residents? In what ways?
2. Have students research and report on the history of CFCs and their impact on ozone depletion.

B. International Controls

The late 1970s saw laws banning CFSs in aerosols in America and Scandinavia.

In 1981, the United Nations approved a plan to develop an international agreement to protect the ozone.
- Delegates from 43 nations met in Vienna at the first international agreement to address CFCs.
- Imposing no controls, the Vienna Convention was signed by 20 countries.
  - The Convention called for countries to take "appropriate measures" to protect the ozone.
  - It also established an international mechanism for research and information exchange.
  - No chemicals were identified as ozone-depleting substances (ODS).

In 1985, two months after negotiations in Vienna ended, British scientists announced an "ozone hole" over Antarctica.
- Their data showed a 50% springtime reduction in the layer compared to the 1960s.
- However, there was no proof at the time that linked CFCs to the ozone hole.

Industry also played a role in the development of controls.
- In 1986, DuPont announced that it could develop CFC substitutes within five years, provided proper regulatory requirements.

In 1987, representatives from over 60 counties met in Montreal to develop the Montreal Protocol, which differed greatly from the Vienna Convention.
- The Montreal Protocol froze production and consumption levels of CFCs.
- Monitoring consumption of ODS was considered impractical, so a formula was adopted to define a country's consumption of CFSs as:

$$consumption = production + imports - exports$$

- The Protocol adopted a "basket" strategy by which each chemical's ozone-depleting potential (ODP) was given a value in relation to that of CFC 11 (which was valued at 1). Countries could determine acceptable reduction rates based on the ODP of each CFC; they could conserve the use of the widely used CFC 113, for instance, by reducing a greater percentage of other CFCs.
- The Protocol also offered strong trade measures as an incentive for countries to join. Parties to the Protocol are not allowed to import certain controlled substances from non-parties, for instance.
- Developing nations were given a ten-year grace period following ratification before implementing control measures.

The Montreal Protocol was considered a great diplomatic triumph, establishing strict international controls where none had previously existed.

C.   Developing Countries

At the time of the original meeting in Montreal, industrialized countries had less than 25% of the population, but consumed 88% of the CFCs—more than 20 times the per capita consumption of developing countries.

Nevertheless, large developing countries such as China and India needed to cooperate with the Protocol.
- Without them, local CFC industries could develop in these nations and never sell products outside their own borders.
- People in these countries viewed CFC-containing products such as refrigerators and air conditioners as necessary to improve their standards of living.
- Developing countries rejected the options of doing without these products or paying for more expensive substitutes.

As a compromise, developed and developing countries approved a funding source—established as the Multilateral Fund in 1992—to support projects and activities in developing countries.
- Example: If it costs a company in India more to use refrigeration technology that does not use CFCs than if traditional refrigeration technologies were used, the Fund would pay for the additional cost of using an ozone-friendly technology.
- By 2008, the Fund had distributed over $2.3 billion to support over 6,000 projects and activities in 148 developing countries.

Suggested Discussion Question
1. Do you agree with providing funding to developing nations to assist them in complying with consumption regulations on CFCs? Why or why not?

D.   *Lessons Learned*

If the Montreal Protocol's reductions are achieved, scientists expect the ozone layer to stabilize by around 2050.

The ozone depletion story offers three primary lessons:
- International environmental challenges cannot be resolved without international cooperation, particularly between developed and developing nations.
- Non-state players, such as scientists and corporations, must also participate in any discussions of potential solutions.
- A precautionary approach to treaty making can work. Rather than relying on unanimous consent before adopting measures, it is best to move ahead incrementally, admitting that more information is needed while not refusing to take action.

III.   Climate Change

A.   *The Science of Climate Change*

It appears that climate change will be the definitive environmental issue of the 21st century.
- Climate change refers to the response of the earth's climate to changes in the concentration of "greenhouse gases" such as CO_2 in the atmosphere.
  - These gases allow sunlight to pass through the atmosphere while absorbing and re-radiating back heat from the earth's surface, warming the planet.
- Policymakers must make decisions on this issue, pitting the world's fossil fuel-based economy against the global climate.

The basic theory of the greenhouse effect was first advanced by Swedish chemist Arrhenius in 1896.
- There is no debate over the warming potential of greenhouse gases.
- The debate concerns how much, at what rate, and where the planet will warm—and how this might affect human health and the environment.

Major man-made (anthropogenic) greenhouse gases include carbon dioxide (CO_2), methane (CH_4), nitrous oxide (NO_x), and chlorofluorocarbons (CFCs).
- Concentrations of these gases have been increasing over the last century, largely as a result of our use of fossil fuels.
- CO_2 and NO_x remain in the atmosphere for decades; current reductions will not reduce their impact for quite a while.

The atmosphere is extremely resilient in adjusting to variations.
- Only about 3 billion of the total 6.5–8.5 billion metric tons of carbon annually emitted into the atmosphere remain there; the rest is assimilated through plants/soil or absorbed by the oceans.
- In addition, many land-use and agricultural practices influence climate change.
  o Carbon sinks remove carbon through the atmosphere (e.g., through photosynthesis).
  o Carbon reservoirs store carbon previously removed from the atmosphere.
  o Forests are probably the best known carbon reservoirs and sinks.

In 1988, the Intergovernmental Panel on Climate Change (IPCC) was created to help build the political will to respond to climate change.

Areas of uncertainty involving climate change still exist, but these areas are narrowing continually.
- International scientists overwhelmingly agree that human activities are in fact changing the earth's climate.
- Long-term climate data suggest the earth's average surface air temperature has increased by 1.37° F (0.74° C) since the 1970s.
  o Areas of greatest warming include Alaska, Siberia, and Antarctica.
  o 2005 was the warmest year on record in the Northern Hemisphere; 2007 tied with 1998 as the second-warmest.
  o Of the twelve years between 1997 and 2008, ten have been the warmest in recorded history.
  o In 2006, Arctic winter ice reached the lowest recorded coverage.
- The IPCC believes that temperatures will increase an additional 1.4° to 5.8° C by 2100 if the trend is not reversed.
- Expected areas of impact: warmer temperatures, stronger storms, sea level rise, water availability, disease, loss of biodiversity

Who is to blame?
- Not all greenhouse gases affect the atmosphere the same way; different gases have different "global warming potentials" (GWPs).
- Most greenhouse gases come from industrial activity. The United States alone has contributed over 30% of historic carbon dioxide emissions.
- The U.S. also has the highest per capita emissions (19.2 metric tons per person annually) among all nations.
- As developing countries increase their industrial activity, greenhouse gas emissions are likely to increase—absent changes in technology.

Suggested Discussion Questions and Activity
1. What are some of the long-term effects of global warming?
2. Is global warming as serious of a problem as some people make it out to be, or is it oversensationalized? Support your answer with data.

3. Have students speak to their parents, grandparents, and other older residents of their community about global warming. How do these people compare today's temperatures and weather patterns with those of their early years?

B.   Impacts of Climate Change

How will climate change affect life on earth?
- Shrinkage of glaciers, thawing of permafrost, lengthening of growing seasons, declines in some plant and animal populations—these are among some of the changes already with us.
- Global sea level has risen between 10–20 cm over the past century, probably because of global warming. Further increases are expected. Possible impacts include shore erosion, altered tidal ranges, increased salinity of estuaries and freshwater aquifers, and increased coastal flooding. Some countries, such as the Maldives and the Cook Islands, could be completely submerged.
- Because warmer temperatures introduce more energy into the global weather system, more extreme weather events are likely: more severe droughts, floods, heat waves; stronger storms and hurricanes; less ice cover.
- Public health is likely to suffer, especially in developing countries. Diseases such as malaria will likely rise, and there will be more deaths from air pollution, heat waves, and so forth.
- Crop yields could vary considerably across regions, increasing in some areas and decreasing in others.
- Loss of biodiversity is likely.

There are some possible benefits as well:
- Increased crop yields in some regions, increased global timber supply, increased water availability in some water-scarce regions, reduced cold-weather deaths.
- Nevertheless, the IPCC has concluded that the costs of climate change will be far greater than the benefits.

Suggested Discussion Activity
1. Divide students into groups and have them debate the costs versus the benefits of combating global warming.

C.   Legal Responses

Calls for international action about climate change began in the 1970s. Negotiations begun by the United Nations in 1990 resulted in 1992's Framework Convention on Climate Change.
- The Climate Change Convention offered few concrete solutions, but it was a first step toward the Kyoto Protocol of 1997.

- The most important provisions of the Climate Change Convention addressed the specific commitments of all parties. Developed (Annex I) countries promised to adopt policies to reduce greenhouse gas emissions to their 1990 levels and enhance sinks and reservoirs, though these were non-binding.

In 1995, an IPCC report identified a strong human influence on global warming. Despite skeptics, many funded by the fossil-fuel industry, this report led directly to the negotiation of the Kyoto Protocol in 1997.

The Kyoto Protocol established binding reduction targets for the United States and other developed countries.
- The core of the Protocol is targets and timetables for countries to reduce their emissions of greenhouse gases.
- Most European countries agreed to lower emissions by 8% below 1990 levels; the U.S. agreed to a 7% reduction.
- Countries in economic transition were allowed to select a baseline year other than 1990.
- Developing nations were not given emission reductions, based on the idea that developed countries produced most greenhouse gases and were in a better position to pay for reductions.
    o These nations are expected to take on reduction targets sometime after 2012.
- The Protocol also establishes broad and general guidance for various "flexibility mechanisms," such as emissions trading and joint implementation.
- Ambiguities in the Protocol were found that could lead to greatly different reduction requirements for developed nations. Nevertheless, all parties recognized the urgency of taking action against emissions.

Suggested Discussion Activity
1. Have students research and write a brief report on the Kyoto Protocol.

D.   *Climate Change Policies—No Regrets, Trading, Joint Implementation, and the CDM*

Several policy options have been developed to reduce the impact of greenhouse gases. International treaties have imposed clear national targets, but have left the methods largely to individual nations.
Policy options can be grouped into two broad categories.
- The goal of a *mitigation approach* is to lower the atmospheric concentration of greenhouse gases, whether through reduced emissions at source or creating new sinks, primarily through land use and forestry management. This is a long-term strategy.
- *Adaptation strategies* address the consequences of climate change and focus on near-term measures that adapt to these changes. Example: Constructing sea walls in low-lying coastal areas to dampen storm surges.

Climate change treaties have primarily focused on mitigation strategies.

Policymakers have generally focused on the "no-regrets" approach.
- These policies involve measures such as improvements in energy efficiency, forest management, and air pollution control. They provide economic/environmental benefits additional to any climate benefits that may result.
- A major problem: No low-cost reliable technology exists for removing CO_2 from fossil-fuel combustion emissions—once it's released, little can prevent the CO_2 from entering the atmosphere.
  o Strategies typically do not include end-of-the-pipe or substitution solutions, as have been used to phase out ozone-depleting substances.

The Kyoto Protocol contains four trading mechanisms (called flexibility mechanisms):
- Emissions trading allows an Annex I party to purchase or transfer part of its assigned amount to another Annex I party in exchange for payment.
- Joint implementation (JI) allows the sale of "reduction units" from one Annex I party or business to another.
  o Reduction units are generated by specific projects that reduce emissions or increase removals in the selling country.
- Joint fulfillment of commitments allows an agreement between two or more parties to meet their combined commitments by reducing their aggregated emissions.
  o This is similar to the bubbling strategy described previously.
- The Clean Development Mechanism (CDM) allows developing countries to help developed countries meet their emission reduction commitments.
  o For example, a developed country could fund activities in a developing country that reduce that country's emissions, and use those reductions to offset their own emissions.

Controversies remain about how to best operate the flexibility mechanisms.
- For example, should countries meet most or at least some of their emission reduction targets at home, or could they simply purchase all of their needed reduction units from another party?

Two main issues have been spotlighted in negotiating "Beyond Kyoto" (the international regime after 2012).
- The first is whether developing countries will take on binding targets.
- The second concerns more explicit land use incentives.
  o Environmentalists have criticized Kyoto because there is no incentive for keeping existing forests intact.
  o Creating carbon credits for "avoided deforestation" (that is, rewarding nations that keep their forests intact) has been proposed as one solution to this problem.

Suggested Discussion Questions
1. Discuss the controversies listed above concerning how to best operate the flexibility mechanisms.
2. What is being done to preserve forests in the United States? Are these methods working? Are they enough?

E.   Sub-National Activity

In 2001, U.S. President George W. Bush declined to submit the Kyoto Protocol to the Senate for ratification.
- The Bush administration largely attempted to reduce greenhouse emissions via voluntary initiatives.
- Seeking to fill the leadership void on this issue, a number of local governments, environmental groups, and businesses have taken their own actions:
  o Litigation—for example, in 2003 the U.S. Department of Energy and Bureau of Land Management were successfully sued for failing to consider CO_2 emissions from power plants in approving construction permits.
  o State regulation—for example, California has enacted a cap-and-trade system designed to reduce greenhouse gas emissions in that state to 1990 levels by 2020.
  o Regional trading schemes—for example, most northeastern states have joined to form the Regional Greenhouse Gas Initiative (RGGI); participating states commit to a 10 percent reduction in carbon dioxide from electricity utilities by 2019, relying on a cap-and-trade system.
  o Corporate initiatives—for example, through the Carbon Disclosure Project, more than 80 per cent of Global 500 companies voluntarily report annual greenhouse gas emissions information.

Suggested Discussion Question
1. Are voluntary initiatives enough to reduce greenhouse emissions? Why or why not? What more could be done?

F.   The Clean Air Act and Climate Change

During the Bush Administration, the Clean Air Act was not used to address climate change because the EPA argued that the CAA did not apply to greenhouse gases.
- This position was challenged in *Massachusetts v.EPA.*
- In 2007, the U.S. Supreme Court made three significant findings in the case:
  o Greenhouse gases are air pollutants under the CAA.
  o The EPA must either issue an endangerment finding under Section 202 or provide a valid reason to decline to do so.
  o In the climate context, sovereign states are owed a "special solicitude" and have a lower threshold for standing than private parties.

Soon into the Obama administration, the EPA issued a proposed endangerment finding under Section 202, a precondition to regulating automobile emissions.

Key question: Does a finding that mobile source emissions of GHGs likely endanger public health or welfare imply that emissions from stationary sources must do the same?
- If so, then three CAA programs are directly implicated –NAAQS/SIPs, NSPS, and the Prevention of Significant Deterioration (PSD) pre-construction permits.

NAAQS/SIPS
- EPA must issue NAAQS in the face of an endangerment finding. But the scale of the greenhouse gas problem and the scale of the NAAQS/SIP structure provide a poor fit.
  - o Because greenhouse gases are a global pollutant, single states have little or no power to reduce greenhouse gases in their airshed.
- In addition, EPA cannot consider costs when implementing regulations. So what is the limiting factor on setting the NAAQS for GHG levels?
  - o Example: Could EPA acknowledge the global nature of greenhouse gases, declare all state SIPs inadequate, and then create a federal implementation program along the lines of a mandatory cap-and-trade program?

NSPS
- The NSPS program is much more flexible than NAAQS, since it potentially allows the EPA to craft greenhouse gas regulation with particular sectors in mind. In theory, this would allow EPA to go slowly and methodically.
- Another advantage of the NSPS program is that, unlike the NAAQS program, it allows EPA to consider costs and take into account the potential drag of regulations on the economy.

PSD
- The PSD program requires pre-construction permits for any new or modified "major" stationary sources. A source is defined as a "major" stationary source if: (i) it is one of the sources explicitly listed in the statute and it emits more than 100 tons of any pollutant regulated under the CAA; or (ii) it emits more than 250 tons of any pollutant regulated under the CAA.
- Since many greenhouse gases are often emitted in much larger amounts than traditional pollutants, emission thresholds would be easily crossed, pushing many emitters into the category of "major stationary sources" for the first time.
- In September 2009, EPA proposed that existing industrial facilities that emit at least 25,000 tons per year of CO_2 must obtain construction and operating permits under Title V. Pre-construction permitting under the PSD program would be required for new sources and existing sources making major modifications that result in emissions of 25,000 tons per year of CO_2.
  - o This was expected to affect about 14,000 large sources of CO_2. Millions of smaller sources would be exempted.

- EPA justified its 100-fold increase in the threshold (i.e., from 250 to 25,000 tons) by claiming the defense of administrative feasibility – the 250-ton threshold would be unworkable because it would cover too many sources.

The Clean Air Act was originally intended as a response to local and regional air pollution, not a global threat such as climate change. Creating a sensible climate policy for the CAA has been difficult.

Some observers believe that the CAA is unfit for the task, and that Congress will be forced to pass climate legislation. But until Congress or the courts say otherwise, the CAA is the law under which we must regulate climate change.

Suggested Discussion Question
1. Is the CAA the best way to regulate climate change? Why or why not? What better mechanisms could be devised?

G.   *Policy Challenges of Climate Legislation*

In late 2009, the House of Representatives passed the Waxman-Markey bill; the Senate was debating its own climate bill. Whatever form the resulting legislation takes, it will be contested and likely amended.

Economists generally prefer regulation of GHGs through the use of carbon taxes, which can be set at the feedstock source and ultimately increases prices for goods dependent on high-GHG fuel sources. However, despite their efficiency, taxes are a politically unpopular solution.

Aversion to taxes—as well as the success of the acid rain trading program—will likely result in climate legislation that relies on an efficient cap-and-trade program.
- A nationwide cap on GHGs is set, emission limits are set for individual sources, and emission allowances are traded such that the overall emissions level reduces over time.
- Two immediately difficult choices:
  - Coverage – which sources in which sectors should be included?
  - Allocation – which sources should be given allowances?

Some observers question whether parties subject to GHG reduction requirements should be able to purchase credits from sequestration projects to offset their emissions.
- Example: Should a coal-fired power plant be able to purchase credits for carbon sequestered by a landowner who has planted 1,000 acres of fast-growing trees?
- Offsets offer multiple benefits:
  - They make compliance less expensive.
  - They bring new segments of the economy into the program.
- However, offsets have some potential problems:

- Monitoring must ensure that the carbon sequestration activities truly are additional to what would have happened anyway.
- Permanence must be also assured; for example, after credits from the forest are sold, the farmer cannot sell the trees for firewood.
- Leakage may occur if a landowner sequesters carbon in one part of his property but increases GHG emissions through land use activities elsewhere.
- Should offsets from abroad count toward domestic reduction obligations?

International competition also raises important issues. Climate legislation could hurt U.S. companies that must compete with foreign manufacturers that do not have to pay for or reduce their GHG emissions.

- To address this concern, climate legislation generally includes variants of what are effectively border taxes. Example: Impose a tariff on imported goods that would reflect the GHGs emitted in their manufacture.
- Climate legislation also uses so-called *safety valves*, which might cap the price of an allowance or rely on a strategic reserve of allowances that can be released to ease supply pressures.

Suggested Discussion Activity

1. Ask students to research and report on the current status of climate legislation in Congress. What arguments are made by opponents of the legislation? What stance is taken toward the legislation by industry? Agricultural groups? Environmental groups? Labor unions?

PART II
Pollution Law

———

CHAPTER 6
Water Pollution

Congress passed the Clean Water Act (CWA) in 1972.
- The CWA has significantly reduced the volume of effluents released from factories and sewage treatment plants into America's waterways. America's waters are much cleaner than when the CWA was originally passed.
- However, there is still much to do to overcome water pollution.
    o A 1996 EPA report revealed that only 22 percent of American watersheds surveyed had "good" water quality; half had "moderate" water quality problems; and the rest suffered "severe" problems.
    o Similar surveys have shown comparable results. For example, 93 percent of the Great Lakes shoreline miles are impaired, primarily from PCBs, toxic organics, and dioxins.

Environmentalists have criticized the CWA.
- It largely ignores hydrological changes to waterways, such as dams and water withdrawals.
- It has done little to prevent runoffs from farms, mines, and other "nonpoint" sources of water pollution.

Economists have also been critical of the CWA.
- It requires factories and other "point" sources of pollution to adopt expensive pollution control technology.
- It does not take a "least cost" approach to improve water quality; by contrast, the CWA typically imposes uniform limitations on all companies within an industry.

I.   An Overview of Water Pollution

There are three main sources of water pollution:
- *Point sources* are factories and other facilities that generally dump pollution directly into waters.
- *Indirect sources* are facilities that empty their wastes into the local sewage system.
- *Nonpoint sources* come from farms, mines, construction sites, and other land uses. Example: When a farmer irrigates crops, much of the water runs off the land and into waterways, taking pesticides and other agricultural chemicals with it.

- o Storm sewers often collect such runoff from city streets and carry it to local streams and rivers.

There are also several other important sources of water pollution.
- Air pollutants are sometimes blown into local waterways
- Atmospheric moisture frequently combines with air pollutants, then deposits the pollution as rain or snow, either directly into waterways or onto land where it runs into water.
  - o Acid rain is one such source of water pollution.
- Water pollution can also arise naturally; many rivers and lakes, for example, are naturally salty.

Changes to the hydrology of a waterway can also affect water quality.
- When water is diverted from a river, there is less water to dilute downstream pollutants.
- Large, artificial reservoirs can increase the evaporation rate and thus increase the concentration of pollutants in the water left behind.
- Dams can change the quality of downstream water.
  - o For instance, water releases from dams often are low in dissolved oxygen, reducing the ability of the water to break down pollutants.

The following are the leading sources of water quality impairment in the United States.
- For rivers and streams: agriculture, hydrologic modification, and urban runoff/storm sewers.
- For lakes: agriculture, hydrologic modification, and urban runoff/storm sewers.
- For estuaries: municipal point sources, urban runoff/storm sewers, industrial facilities, and agriculture.
- As can be seen, nonpoint sources are greater causes of water pollution than most point sources—largely because the CWA has done a poor job of regulating such sources.

Suggested Discussion Question and Activity
1. Are you aware of water pollution problems in your community? What is being done to control those problems?
2. Have students visit the EPA's web site to learn more about the Clean Water Act.

II. A Brief History of Water Quality Regulation

Well into the 20th century, the regulation of surface water pollution was mostly regulated by American courts.
- By the 1930s, most states had water pollution control programs, but they were generally poorly enforced.
  - o States were reluctant to impose the expense of cleanup onto local governments.

- o They also feared driving industry elsewhere if they seriously attempted to regulate industrial discharges.
- o Nonpoint pollution was not addressed at all.

Congress first addressed water pollution in the 1965 Water Quality Act.
- It relied almost entirely on the states for enforcement.
- States were required to designate intended uses for interstate waterways (e.g., drinking water, swimming, aquatic life support, etc.).
- States were also required to develop water quality plans and standards to ensure that each classification of waterway met its intended use.
- The Act failed to control water pollution.
  - o States lacked the political will to meet quality standards.
  - o Technical problems doomed enforcement: most states did not have the means to determine appropriate standards for any particular waterway use. Even if they had the means, they lacked the ability to translate standards into effluent standards for individual pollution sources.
  - o Polluters often argued that their discharges were not the cause of water quality problems; states could not demonstrate otherwise.

By 1970, America's water problems had become severe.
- About 50% of states had not developed standards under the 1965 Water Quality Act.
- Fewer than 10% of all municipal sewage plants used anything other than filters and settling tanks to treat sewage.
- Less than 1/3 of industrial facilities treated wastes before dumping them into waterways.
- Some scientists feared that certain waterways, such as Lake Erie, were beyond hope. (Ohio's Cuyahoga River, near Cleveland, had actually caught fire in 1969.)

Suggested Discussion Question and Activity
1. Discuss with students some of the water pollution standards in your state.
2. Have someone from your local water and sewage plant visit the classroom and talk about the technologies used to treat water and sewage in your community.

III. The Clean Water Act

Congress passed the Clean Water Act (CWA) in 1972.
- Goals of the Act were to:
  - o Protect marine life and permit water recreation.
  - o Eliminate all discharges of pollution into America's waterways by 1985.
- Critics of the Act, including the National Water Commission, argued that:
  - o The Act's goals were infeasible and would only disappoint the public.
  - o The Act's "no discharge" goal implied that perfectly pure water was a desirable goal worth whatever it cost to obtain it.

The CWA has not even remotely met its goals. So why were such extravagant goals set in the first place?

- Congress may have wanted to emphasize the seriousness of water pollution.
- Congress may have believed that ambitious goals were needed to ensure the proper level of commitment toward solving the problem

There are three main categories of water quality provisions in the CWA:

- The most important regulations center on point sources of pollution.
- A second set of provisions—to date, far less consequential—requires states to develop plans to regulate nonpoint pollution.
- A final set of provisions—becoming increasingly relevant—requires states to set water standards for waterways within their borders and to limit discharges as needed to achieve them.
- Other regulatory provisions also exist; for example, the filling of wetlands is restricted.

The CWA applies only to "navigable waters," but defines the term generously to mean— essentially—all waters in the United States.

- Courts have concluded that, in most cases, the CWA generally does not apply to groundwater.

Suggested Discussion Question
1. Why do you think the CWA has failed to meet its goals?

A.   Regulation of Point Sources

The main goal of the CWA was to reduce discharges from point sources. This could have been achieved in many different ways.

- Congress could have set water quality standards for the entire nation, then left it to the states to find ways to meet them.
  - o But problems related to the 1965 Water Quality Act showed that states would find it difficult to accomplish this.
- Therefore, Congress decided to have the EPA establish effluent limitations for each type of point source.
  - o This eliminates the need to determine what levels of pollution are consistent with various water uses.
  - o States simply apply existing technology to each individual point source.
- Essentially, the CWA reverses the procedure of the CAA: It begins with individual effluent levels rather than ambient water concentrations.

1.   NPDES Permits

Congress implements technological limitations through the National Pollutant Discharge Elimination System (NPDES).

- Under the CWA, no one can discharge pollutants into waterways without an NPDES permit.
  - "Discharge of a pollutant" is defined as "any addition of any pollutant to navigable waters from any point source."
- NPDES permits are good for five years, after which they must be renewed.

The NPDES approach allows very effective enforcement.
- Each point source must report discharges on a regular (usually monthly) basis to the EPA.
- The reports are admissible as evidence in court.
- The permits and reports are public records, so anyone can check for violations.
- This came into play in the 1980s when private citizens trained by the Natural Resources Defense Council examined permits and reports and began checking for CWA violations (which the Reagan administration was reluctant to prosecute).

Suggested Discussion Activity
1. Have students write a brief report on NPDES permits. The EPA web site is a good place to start for researching the topic.

2.   Publicly Owned Treatment Works

Effluent limitations in an NPDES permit depend on whether the permit holder is a sewage plant (publicly owned treatment work, or POTW) or another type of point source.
- The CWA requires POTWs to use a specific level of technology.

There are three broad categories of sewage treatment technology:
- Primary treatment: POTWs separate out solid from liquid waste using filters, screens, and settlement tanks.
- Secondary treatment: POTWs use microorganisms to biologically break down organic matter.
- Tertiary treatment: POTWs "polish" away remaining contaminants through physical means such as sand filters or membrane microfiltration.

Originally, the CWA required all POTWs to use secondary treatment by 1977; by 1983, they were to use "the best practicable waste treatment technology over the life of the works."
- Congress authorized funds to help municipalities upgrade their POTWs.
- However these provisions largely failed.
  - Many cities were still not using secondary treatment by 1977.
  - Costs of converting to secondary treatment were even higher than anticipated.
  - Many cities used federal funds to expand their sewage systems rather than improve effluent quality. Federal budget constraints impeded continuing funding anyway.

Given the failures, Congress amended the CWA to eliminate the 1983 standard and—in some cases—even to waive the 1977 standard.

3.   Industrial Point Sources

Point sources other than POTWs must meet technology-based effluent limits.
- Unlike POTWs, these sources are not required to use a particular technology; they must simply meet the effluent limitations.
- Most sources adopt the technology used by the EPA to determine limitation levels since they know it will allow them to meet the standards.

Which technology should the EPA use to determine effluent limitations?
- First, *what types* of technology should be considered?
    - End-of-pipe technologies help clean up industrial byproducts before they are discharged.
    - Pollution prevention technologies can help facilities reduce their discharges by changing their industrial processes themselves.
    - But most companies resist efforts to regulate their processes:
        1. Process changes can be more expensive than end-of-pipe technology.
        2. Regulation of process is considered unwanted government intrusion into business.
        3. Process changes are less certain to meet effluent limits than end-of-pipe technologies.
        4. Process changes can negatively affect product quality.
- Second, *how* should the government choose the technology?
    - By a cost-benefit comparison?
    - By its affordability?
    - Because of economic feasibility?
    - Based simply on whether the technology works, regardless of cost?
- Third, *on what basis* should limitations be determined: facility-by-facility or industry-by-industry?

The CWA does not consistently approach these issues.
- Congress has set standards in different ways based on whether facilities are old or new or on the type of pollution being discharged.
- The various standards can be summarized as follows:
    - BPT—end-of-pipe technology/cost compared to benefit
    - BCT—end-of-pipe technology/cost can be considered
    - BAT—end-of-pipe technology/cost can be considered
    - BCT—end-of-pipe technology as well as process and operation changes/no consideration of cost

4. Existing Point Sources

The CWA originally provided that effluent limitations for existing point sources should reflect the "best practicable control technology currently available" (BPT) by 1977; by 1983, the "best available technology economically achievable" (BAT) was to be used.

- Congress anticipated that BAT would be the more stringent of the two standards.
- Congress also believed that a technological approach was not appropriate when a point source discharged toxic pollutants.
    - o In these cases, effluent limitations should protect human health, no matter the difficulty or cost to the point source.

Industry objections forced Congress to abandon the universal BAT standard to all existing point sources, as well as its health-based approach to toxic pollutants.

- Today, the technological standard that the EPA uses to set effluent limitations depends on the type of pollution the source releases:
    - o Toxic pollutants—a list of 126 chemicals determined to be toxic.
        1. Because scientists have only recently begun to understand the health risks associated with various pollutants, the health-based approach has been abandoned entirely.
        2. The BAT standard is now used to calculate effluent limitations for this category of pollutant.
    - o Conventional pollutants—commonly used pollutants such as suspended solids, pH, oil, and grease.
        1. Instead of the BAT standard, the EPA now sets limitations for these pollutants based on the "best conventional pollutant control technology" (BCT).
    - o Nonconventional pollutants—pollutants not fitting into the other two categories (e.g., ammonia, color, iron).
        1. These substances are generally subject to the BAT standard, though waivers are sometimes allowed.

Suggested Discussion Question
1. What common household products fall into the category of conventional pollutants? Do you think about controlling these pollutants when you use and dispose of these products?

5. New Point Sources

Like the CAA, the CWA imposes stricter effluent limitations on new industrial point sources.

- Policy perspective: New sources do not need to retrofit their facilities (which can be expensive); they can build pollution control into their design.
- Political perspective: Existing sources usually lobby against stringent discharge standards, while few companies worry about hypothetical future plants.
    - o In fact, existing companies often support strict standards for new point sources, since they can be a barrier to new entries into the marketplace.

Stricter standards present some problems, however:
- In theory, they can reduce the number of companies competing in any given industry.
- The reduced competition can lead to higher product prices or monopolies.
- Companies may have an incentive to keep their existing plants, which tend to be bigger polluters.

Under the CWA, new point sources must meet standards that reflect the "best available control technology, processes, operating methods, or other alternatives, including, where practicable, a standard permitting no discharge of pollutants" (BCT).

Suggested Discussion Question
1. Do you think new companies should have strict standards for controlling water pollution? List the pros and cons of strict standards for new companies.

6. Industry-by-Industry Determination

The CWA does not state whether effluent limitations apply on a facility-by-facility basis or an industry-by-industry basis.
- In 1977, the Supreme Court ruled that the EPA could set industry-wide guidelines.
- As a result, the EPA now has set standards for more than 50 major categories of industrial facilities.
- Companies dissatisfied with the guidelines must challenge them when issued by the EPA, not when the government uses them to set effluent limitations in individual NPDES permits.

Industrial plants that believe they are different from most of the competitors in their industry can apply for variances from the industry-wide standards.
- Point sources can apply for a "fundamentally different factor" (FDF) variance.
  - FDF variances cannot be issued on the basis of cost factors; applicants must show that the applicable technology will not work because of unique characteristics of the facility. (Example: A fish cannery located in the mountains rather than on a coastline.)
- Point sources can also get variances from the BCT limits for conventional pollutants because they do not have the economic means to meet the national standard or because less stringent limitations will still adequately protect waterways.

Suggested Discussion Activity
1. Divide students into groups of three and four. Have each group choose a specific industry and research the pollution guidelines for that industry. Have each group report their findings to the class.

7. Indirect Sources

Companies frequently try to avoid effluent limitation requirements, often by discharging the waste into the local sewage system rather than directly into a waterway. This presents two main problems:

- The secondary treatment required of most POTWs does not adequately treat a number of industrial pollutants.
- Industrial pollution can increase the risk of fire or explosion at a POTW and can interfere with the treatment of other waste.

To address these problems, the CWA regulates indirect sources of pollution in two ways:

- Prohibited discharge standards—Waste cannot be discharged into a POTW system if it will interfere with the operation of the POTW or pass through untreated.
- Categorical pretreatment standards—Indirect sources must meet BAT standards for any discharge of pollutants into a POTW system (unless the POTW can treat them adequately).
- In addition, most POTWs impose their own limits on what forms of industrial wastes they will accept.

8. Criticism of the Technological Approach

Economists have been critical of the CWA's technological approach because it does not take the most cost-effective route to reducing water pollution.

- Generally, all facilities in the same industry must meet the same standards, even if pollution from one is not as harmful as pollution from another.
- In addition, an industry with minimal impact on water quality might need to spend more money than an industry with severe water pollution issues.
- Economists generally believe that the focus should be on those facilities where the net benefits are greatest.
- Economic studies suggest that technological standards have cost too much: A 1990 study estimated that costs through 1985 were between $25–30 billion, with benefits between $6–28 billion.

Environmentalists have also criticized the CWA's approach.

- The EPA often takes years to develop and adopt standards, and has frequently missed deadlines for the issuance of standards.
- Environmentalists believe the EPA should focus more on the effects of water pollution on human and aquatic health, rather than on engineering questions.

But the CWA's technological standards have, in fact, reduced water pollution in the United States. They work, and they are easy to enforce. That is why they are used.

1. Why do you think the costs of implementing technological standards far exceed the benefits? Is it worth continuing to implement these standards if the costs are so high?

B.   The Non-Regulation of Nonpoint Sources

Despite the CWA's successful regulation of point sources, it has done a poor job with nonpoint pollution.
- In practice, the CWA leaves regulation of nonpoint sources up to the states.
- Section 208 of the CWA requires states to designate agencies to attempt to control pollution in waterways with "substantial water quality problems" by developing waste treatment management plans.
- States are not required to implement these plans, however.
- Agricultural, mining, and construction lobbies have convinced most states not to adopt water quality plans to any significant degree.

By the mid-1980s, nonpoint pollution had become the largest source of water pollution in the United States.
- As a result, section 319 was added to the CWA in 1987, requiring states to implement a "nonpoint source management program."
- States must also require nonpoint sources to use BMPs as early as possible.
- However, Congress has not enforced section 319 in any meaningful way.

Why has Congress been unwilling to attempt to reduce nonpoint pollution?
- Nonpoint sources are often more difficult to find than point sources.
- There are many more nonpoint than point sources, and they are more varied, complicating efforts toward solutions.
- Land uses have traditionally been left to states and local governments.
- However, none of these problems should prevent action.
    - Under a BMP approach, the government would not necessarily even need to monitor pollution, simply whether sources are using the mandated BMPs.

Essentially, politics—particularly the agriculture lobby—has been behind the CWA's failure to take on nonpoint pollution.

Suggested Discussion Questions
1. What are some ways to combat nonpoint pollution?
2. Why aren't states more proactive in trying to control nonpoint pollution?

C. Escaping Regulation as a Point Source of Pollutants

When there is a distinction between two different types of activities, and one is regulated more than the other, it is inevitable that the regulated community will attempt to cross the line into the more unregulated territory.

To escape NPDES regulation, many potential regulatory targets have argued about the meaning of certain phrases, such as "point source" or whether it is "adding" a "pollutant" to a waterway.

1. What Is a Point Source?

One of the most important questions in the early years of the CWA revolved around whether or not agricultural runoff could be considered a point source.
- Based on original CWA definitions, it should be.
- Nevertheless, in 1973 the EPA exempted farms of less than 3,000 acres, as well as animal feedlots and silviculture, from the NPDES permit requirements.
- The EPA also argued that it would be overwhelmed by the sheer number of agricultural sources if it were forced to monitor them.

The EPA was sued over its decision.
- In *Natural Resources Defense Council v. Costle*, the D.C. Circuit Court invalidated the EPA's decision.
    - But shortly thereafter, Congress amended the definition of point source to exclude return flows from irrigated agriculture.
    - Agriculture lobbyists convinced Congress to prohibit the EPA from requiring an NPDES permit for discharges consisting entirely of return flow from irrigated agriculture.

In 1987, Congress did bring some forms of storm water runoff under the NPDES system.

Suggested Discussion Questions
1. Should agriculture be considered a point source? Why or why not?
2. Why do you think the EPA and Congress have been lenient in forcing the agriculture industry to control water pollution?

2. When Does a Point Source "Add" "Pollutants"?

Hydrologic modifications of rivers and other waterways are major sources of water pollution.
- They contribute to pollution in about 26% of America's impaired rivers and streams, 17% of its lakes, and 10% of its estuaries.
- Given this, it has been debated as to whether such modifications require NPDES permits.

o   Dams clearly meet the definition of a point source; however, courts have uniformly held that dams do not "add" "pollutants."
o   Other types of water projects also sometimes come under scrutiny. Example: Draining the Everglades for farming—must the government get an NPDES permit before discharging the water at its new point of destination?

In *South Florida Water Management District v. Miccosukee Tribe*, Native American groups and environmentalists argued that such a permit was, in fact, needed for the water district to pump water from a canal containing pollutants into an undeveloped wetland.
- The federal government claimed that the permit was not needed because such a transfer does not "add" pollutants to the navigable waters of the U.S.
- The Supreme Court declined to rule, because it was not clear if the canal and wetlands were "distinct water bodies" with no hydrologic connections.

Other courts, however, have ruled that some water transfers do require NPDES permits.
- Example: New York City was required to obtain a permit before discharging water from Schoharie Reservoir into the "naturally clearer and cooler" Esopus Creek.

D.   Water Quality Standards

Even though the CWA takes a largely technological approach to water pollution, it retained water quality standards as a backup to the technology-based effluent limitations.

Section 303 of the CWA sets out a multi-step process for regulating ambient water quality:
- First, each state designates specific beneficial uses for each of its waterways.
- Second, states determine the water quality standards needed to support the designated uses.
- Finally, the states must identify quality-limited waterways: those where the technology-based effluent limitations do not attain the necessary water quality standards.
  o   For each quality-limited waterway, states must determine the total maximum daily load (TMDL) of pollutants that can be dumped into the waterway and still meet the standard.

It is unclear what happens after a state establishes TMDLs.
- Must a state reduce nonpoint pollution if needed to achieve designated water quality standards? The CWA does not say.
- For the first 25 years of the CWA, states did not prepare TMDLs for their quality-limited waterways—and were not forced to do so by the EPA.

However, since the mid-1980s, courts have pressured the EPA to take TMDLs more seriously.

- Example: In 2002, courts held that states must set TMDLs for a waterway that does not meet appropriate standards even if only nonpoint sources pollute it.

Concentrations of pollutants can be reduced either by reducing the pollution entering the waterway or by increasing the amount of water and diluting the pollution.
- Some have suggested augmenting the flow of quality-impaired waterways to meet water quality standards (flow augmentation).
- Environmentalists claim flow augmentation simply masks pollution, and the CWA prohibits the federal government from releasing water from federal water projects for this purpose
- The EPA regulations allow flow augmentation in some settings, however.

E.   *Always Cleaner, Never Dirtier*

The CWA suggests that technology-based limitations should become progressively more rigorous.

In most cases, the CWA also prohibits states from modifying NPDES permits to allow more pollution. In only two cases would a more lenient permit be issued:
- If new information demonstrates that a lower technology-based standard is appropriate.
- If a point source cannot meet its NPDES requirements despite installation and operation of appropriate control equipment.

The CWA's water quality provisions also include an "antidegradation" policy.
- States must protect water quality where waterways are meeting their designated uses.
- States cannot permit the degradation of high-quality waters unless they can prove an economic or social justification for doing so.

F.   *Water Quality Trading*

Though the CWA does not explicitly provide for pollution trading along the lines of the CAA, over the past decade EPA has encouraged states to create and use water quality trading programs.

In the simplest trading programs, a point source that "over controls" its discharge of a particular pollutant receives a credit that it can sell to another point source that cannot cost-effectively reduce its pollution.
- This creates two potential advantages:
  - Overall cost is reduced by allowing companies that can inexpensively reduce their pollution to generate credits that enable other companies facing higher discharge-control costs to avoid or reduce those costs.
  - Trading programs can encourage the development and use of new and better control technologies.

Some believe that TMDLs offer an opportunity for point and nonpoint sources to engage in trading.
- However, a reduction in discharges at one point in a waterway is not necessarily equivalent to a reduction somewhere else along the line.

Limitations such as these have hindered the growth of water quality trading.
- Between 1995–2008, the number of trading schemes increased from eight to almost one hundred—but one of those programs accounts for 80% of the trades.

Suggested Discussion Question
1. Are any water quality trading programs in place in your state? Do you think that water quality trading has a viable future? Why or why not?

G. Interstate Water Pollution

Interstate waters have been a point of controversy since the founding of the United States.

Downstream states have few ways to protect themselves from pollution discharged in upstream states. Yet the CWA pays little attention to the problem of interstate pollution.

The CWA's ambient water quality provisions may be the best means of protection for downstream states.

The EPA will probably not get involved in situations unless discharges would cause a clear deterioration in water quality in the downstream state.

The CWA has reduced states' ability to deal with water pollution from other states in at least one way.
- In 1972, the Supreme Court ruled that a state could sue another to reduce pollution under the "federal common law" of nuisance.
- However, almost ten years later, in the *Milwaukee II* decision, the Court held that the CWA preempts such federal common law actions.
- Six years after *Milwaukee II*, the Court ruled that a Vermont resident could not use Vermont nuisance law to prevent discharges that occurred in New York State.

Suggested Discussion Question
1. Is your state a victim of interstate pollution? What is being done to protect your state from interstate pollution?

PART II
Pollution Law

CHAPTER 7
Regulating Toxic Substances

The CAA and CWA both focus on "conventional" pollutants, but many people are even more concerned with toxic substances.
- Definition of toxic: Products and by-products that present a potential risk of serious harm even at low exposure levels.
- Rachel Carson's book *Silent Spring*—which helped begin the modern environmental era—discussed the dangers of toxic pollution such as pesticides, not conventional pollution.
- Toxic substances such as lead and asbestos tend to worry people far more than any side effects of conventional pollution.

Toxic substances are different from conventional pollutants in many important ways.
- Many of them are valuable agricultural, industrial, or consumer products, not simply by-products that can easily be done without.
- Scientists often are unsure about the risks of specific toxins.
- The probability that a toxin will injure any one individual is usually very low.
- Because even low exposure levels can harm human health, safe exposure levels to many toxins do not exist.

Many federal statutes address toxic substances.
- The CAA and CWA include measures that regulate toxins.
- The Resource Conservation and Recovery Act (RCRA) and Comprehensive Environmental Response, Compensation, and Liability Act (CERCLA) focus on disposal of hazardous waste and clean-up of contaminated land.
- Several statutes, such as the Federal Insecticide, Fungicide, and Rodentcide Act (FIFRA), regulate specific categories of toxins.
- Other laws, such as the Occupational Safety and Health Act (OSHA), regulate specific routes of exposure.
- The Toxic Substances Control Act (TSCA) is a "catch all" statute covering the production, sale, and use of toxins not otherwise regulated by federal law.

Suggested Discussion Questions and Activities
1. Read and discuss some excerpts from *Silent Spring*, by Rachel Carson, with the class.
2. Have students name some common toxins that have been of recent concern.

3. Divide students into groups of three or four, and assign each group one of the federal statutes that address toxic substances. Have each group research its assigned statute and report back to the class on details such as when it was passed, what it regulates, etc.

I. The Difficulties of Regulating Toxic Substances

The regulation of toxins has proven complicated, due largely because of the difficult questions such regulation engenders.

- Life is not risk-free, so should the government be concerned about the low risk levels posed by many toxins?
- What should be the "trigger point" for regulation, given the low level of risk?
- How should the law deal with scientific uncertainty, and in the face of uncertainty should the government favor the economy or public health?
- How much money should be spent to handle such potentially small risks?

If toxic substances were not valuable, these questions would be easy to answer. But many toxins are considered "indispensable" to our modern society.

- Examples: Pesticides allow farmers to dramatically increase their crop yields; chemicals have produced life-saving drugs; the chemical industry employs over 1 million Americans and generates billions to the U.S. economy.

A. Is "Tolerable Risk" an Oxymoron?

Most toxins present only a *risk* of injury.

- Example: For every 1 million people exposed to a carcinogen (cancer-causing substance), perhaps only two will actually contract cancer as a result.
- Is that enough of a risk to regulate the substance, especially if it is economically valuable?
- The natural world contains many health risks, and people often assume additional risks.
  - o Our food contains many natural carcinogens.
  - o We drive in cars, fly in planes, and so forth, which are potentially risky behaviors.
  - o Should government regulate chemicals that are less risky than these common activities?

Some people argue that government should regulate *only* those substances that pose risks *greater* than people assume in their daily lives.

- However, risks vary in a number of important aspects—in addition to their likelihood of occurring.
  - o Different risks pose different types of threats. Example: Some forms of death are feared more than others (e.g., cancer vs. heart attack).
  - o People view voluntary risks differently than risks that are imposed on them.

- o Some risks may be less equitable than others. Example: People are less willing to accept the risk of an accident that could kill 1,000 people in a single location (e.g., nuclear accident) than a risk that could kill 1,000 people spread out over the entire nation (lung disease caused by factory fumes).
- In regulating risks, then, it is not enough simply to know the probability of harm.

Congress, as the elected "voice of the people," seems best suited to determine acceptable risk levels.
- In many cases, Congress has in fact faced up to that challenge.
- But in other instances, it has failed to resolve tensions between economic interests on one hand and health concerns on the other.

The Supreme Court addressed the issue of "acceptable" risk in *Industrial Union Department, AFL-CIO v. American Petroleum Institute* (aka the *Benzene Case*).
- OSHA allows the Secretary of Labor to regulate workplace exposure to toxic materials.
  - o Section 6(b)(5) of OSHA specifies an exposure standard that "*most adequately assures* . . . that *no* employee will suffer material impairment of health or functional capacity."
  - o By contrast, Section 3(8) of OSHA states that the standards should be "*reasonably* necessary or appropriate to provide *safe* or healthful employment and places of employment."
- In the late 1970s, the Department of Labor lowered the exposure level for benzene, a substance known to cause leukemia, concluding that no known level of benzene exposure was safe.
- The Supreme Court reversed the decision, concluding that OSHA requires only those levels of exposure that present a "significant risk of material health impairment" to be banned.
  - o The Court ruled that OSHA requires only a "safe" workplace, not a "risk-free" workplace.
  - o A concurring opinion further concluded that OSHA was unconstitutional because it delegates to an administrative agency a legislative decision about an appropriate level of protection. In other words, this should be Congress's call—not the Department of Labor's.
- A dissenting opinion asserted that the Court's decision ignored the broad discretion given the Secretary of Labor to protect workers' health.

Suggested Discussion Activity
1. Divide the class in half and have them debate the pros and cons of regulating carcinogens that are also economically valuable.

B.   *The Problem of Uncertainty*

Scientific uncertainty also stymies efforts to regulate toxins.
- Difference between risk and uncertainty:

- o If scientists know that exposure to a substance will cause cancer in 2 of every 1,000 people, there would be risk but little uncertainty.
- o If scientists suspect that everyone who consumes X amount of a substance will contract cancer, but they do not have enough information to be sure, there would be uncertainty.
  - 1. If subsequent studies confirmed that the substance was carcinogenic, there would be certitude rather than risk of injury.
- Risk and uncertainty combine to make regulation difficult.

1. A Paucity of Information

One reason behind the difficulty of regulating toxins is that we have not studied many of them carefully.
- In 1984, the National Academy of Sciences concluded that toxicity information about most chemicals was "scanty." Not much has changed since.

Businesses worldwide manufacture over 10 million different chemicals, and thousands more are discovered each year.
- Performing safety tests on all of these would be time consuming and very expensive.

The federal government generally requires companies to test only those categories of chemicals that are of high concern because of their general characteristics or proposed use. Examples:
- FIFRA requires toxicology tests on all new pesticides and agricultural chemicals.
- Federal Food Drug & Cosmetic Act requires tests of chemicals added to food or cosmetics.

By contrast, TSCA does not automatically require extensive tests on new chemicals.
- Companies must file a pre-manufacture notification (PMN) with the EPA before manufacturing a new chemical showing that it "will not present an unreasonable risk."
- But TSCA does not mandate specific testing. No toxicity information accompanies about half of the PMNs.
- Section 4 of TSCA authorizes the EPA to require tests under certain circumstances, but in practice this rarely occurs.

Even mandated tests are not always extensive.
- Example: FIFRA requires testing of the carcinogenic risks of chemicals, but not of some other potential risks.

Suggested Discussion Question
1. Why do you think the effects of toxins haven't been studied more?

2.   The Difficulty of Determining Cancer Risks

Even exhaustive tests would not reveal the exact health risks of many chemicals, especially carcinogens.

Generally, there are two main methods of determining the cancer risks of a chemical: epidemiological studies and animal bioassays.

- Epidemiological studies: Scientists examine populations of humans who have been exposed to a substance to see if they suffer a greater incidence of cancer than the general population.
    - o Because humans must have been exposed to a substance to conduct such a study, they don't help determine if a *new* chemical is carcinogenic.
    - o Even substances on the market for years are difficult to test, because exposure today might not manifest itself as cancer for 20+ years.
- Animal bioassay: Researchers expose laboratory animals to substances and then observe whether the exposed animals suffer a greater incidence of cancer than the unexposed animals.
    - o But if a substance causes cancer in rats or mice, does that mean it will cause it in humans?
    - o How is animal exposure translated into human exposure? Exposing a rat to 2 milligrams of benzene a day is not equivalent to exposing a person to the same amount.
    - o Animals are usually exposed to "mega-doses" of substances—far more than humans would ever likely be exposed to.
- In addition to these two types of studies, scientists have been using *in vitro* cell and tissue cultures to study potential risks of chemicals.
    - o Such tests are cheaper than epidemiological studies and animal bioassays, but their accuracy is disputed.

Even if scientists correctly understand the risk of various substances, the government would still be responsible for determining exposure levels.

Suggested Discussion Question
1. Discuss the reliability of epidemiological studies and animal bioassays. Do these methods of determining cancer risks provide enough reliable information to warrant doing them?

3.   Regulating Under Uncertainty

Because of the scientific uncertainty surrounding toxicity levels, the government's ability to meet a burden of proof is especially important.

- Government is likely to regulate fewer substances if it must prove that something is "unsafe," than if producers must prove that it is "safe."

The standard of proof is also key.

- Scientists usually demand a high level of certainty—up to 90 or 95 percent—before concluding that a substance poses a serious heath risk.
- The law will usually act with far less certainty. Example: *Reserve Mining Co. v. EPA.*
  - In this case, the federal government wanted to prevent Reserve Mining Company from discharging taconite into Lake Superior.
  - Because health studies surrounding taconite were inconclusive at the time, a panel of the Eight Circuit Court of Appeals ruled that the government had not met its burden of proof regarding the substance's danger.
  - Rehearing the case en banc, however, the Eighth Circuit disagreed with the panel, ruling that the government need only show a "reasonable medical concern for the public health."
- The D.C. Circuit ruled similarly for the government in *Ethyl Corp. v. EPA.*

Precautionary regulation can be difficult to sustain over the long run.
- Under precautionary regulation, the government will regulate some substances that will turn out later to be safe.
- Such regulation is often cited as evidence of government over-regulation.

Suggested Discussion Question
1. Should the government use precautionary regulation of toxins? In this case, is it "better to be safe than sorry"?

II.   Major Regulatory Options

Government has used many approaches to regulate toxins.
- First, government must decide whether to ban/limit the production of the toxin, or to permit production but control exposure.
- Second, government must decide the appropriate regulatory standard.
  - A *health-based approach* bans all risks or all significant risks.
  - A *feasibility approach* reduces risks or significant risks only to a level of technological and economic achievability.
  - A *risk-benefit approach* regulates substances only when their risks outweigh their benefits to society.
- Risk-benefit analysis is usually—but not always—the most lenient.

A.   Pure Health-Based Statutes

Congress has not often banned all risks in a class of substances. The most famous examples are the Delaney Clauses in the Federal Food, Drug, and Cosmetic Act.
- The Clauses require government to treat additives as unsafe if they are "found . . . to induce cancer in man or animal."
- Courts have refused to let administrative agencies create a de minimis exception to the Clauses.

- In *Public Citizen v. Young*, the FDA refused to ban two color additives to cosmetics because the risks were "so trivial as to be effectively no risk." The D.C. Circuit Court did not allow the FDA's action.

The Delaney Clauses have been criticized as inflexible and irrational.
- Critics see no reason to ban substances that present only trivial risks.
- Such extreme regulation may lead some agencies to ignore the statute.
- Clauses could backfire by rigidly regulating some but not all risks.
  - Example: A cosmetic manufacturer may not add a substance with a negligible cancer risk but may substitute a substance with a greater risk of other injury.

Defenders of the Delaney Clauses counter the critics' arguments.
- Scientific uncertainty surrounding cancer risks requires a precautionary approach.
  - Defenders assert that most risks have turned out to be worse than scientists originally thought (though there seems to be no convincing evidence regarding this claim).
- Few additives are valuable and so can be easily eliminated.
- The public highly values regulation of even small cancer risks.

But the Delaney Clauses can sometimes be illogical.
- Example: Until 1996, pesticide residues were banned from canned vegetables but not raw foods.
  - The Food Quality Protection Act of 1996 finally extended protection to raw foods (though it also lowered the standard of protection in processed foods.)

Suggested Discussion Activity
1. Have students research the Delaney Clauses. Then divide the class into two groups—one will be critics and one will be defenders—and have them debate the Delaney Clauses.

B.   Feasibility Statutes

Other statues regulate toxic health risks only to a "feasible" degree. For example, OSHA takes this standard in regulating workplace exposures.
- Recall the *Benzene Case* cited earlier.

The Safe Drinking Water Act (SDWA) also takes the feasibility approach.
- The EPA sets maximum containment level goals (MCLGs) for contaminants in public water systems—these are often set at zero because scientists do not know if there is a safe level for most carcinogens.
- Rather than force water suppliers to meet these goals, though, OSHA requires the EPA to establish "maximum containment levels" (MCLs) that are as close to the MCLGs as possible. Suppliers must meet these MCLs, not MCLGs.

Feasibility standards can sometimes lead to arbitrary distinctions.
- Example: Workers in economically precarious industries could be subject to high risks because the industries cannot afford to reduce the risks, while workers in prosperous industries enjoy freedom even from minor risks.

Such standards can also be hard to implement.
- OSHA has estimated that a feasibility review for each new exposure standard takes one year and costs hundreds of thousands of dollars.
- Plus, much of the information to determine feasibility comes from the industries themselves, which naturally often overstate the time and cost involved.

Economists are not convinced that feasibility requirements ensure that the benefits are always "worth" the cost.

Suggested Discussion Question
1. Are feasibility reviews worth their costs? Support your opinion.

C.   Risk-Benefit Statutes

1.   Federal Insecticide, Fungicide, and Rodentcide Act

FIFRA is a classic risk-benefit statute. It requires pesticide or agricultural chemical manufacturers to register new substances with the EPA before producing and selling them.

Under FIFRA, the EPA must determine:
- That the substance will do what the manufacturer claims.
- That the substance will not pose an "unreasonable" risk to humans or the environment when used properly, taking economic, social, and environmental costs into account.

If the substance presents an unreasonable risk, the EPA can refuse to register it or restrict how it is used.
- To date, over 50,000 agricultural chemicals have been registered under FIFRA.

Many substances that seemed safe years ago now seem suspect after further scientific review.
- So FIFRA requires the EPA to periodically reevaluate and re-register existing products.
- It also allows the EPA to cancel a substance's registration or use conditions if warranted.
  - Congress originally required the EPA to reimburse users and manufacturers for the cost of canceling a substance; in 1988, the requirement to indemnify manufacturers was eliminated.

Suggested Discussion Question

1. Do some students prefer to eat only organically grown fruits and vegetables? Are they willing to pay more for these? Why are other students not so worried about eating fruits and vegetables that were sprayed with pesticides?

2.   Toxic Substances Control Act

TSCA is also a risk-benefit statute.
- It requires manufacturers of substances not otherwise regulated to file a pre-manufacturing notice (PMN) before producing and selling the chemical.
- TSCA chemicals are usually not as hazardous as pesticides, so the EPA must not evaluate risks for every chemical for which a PMN is filed.
  - The EPA can ban or restrict the use of substances that it "reasonably" concludes pose a major risk, balancing benefits against the risks.

3.   "Paralysis by Analysis"

Many environmentalists worry that statutes like FIFRA and TSCA lead to "paralysis by analysis." In other words, the EPA spends so much time studying a problem that the problem is really not addressed adequately.

Example: *Corrosion Proof Fittings v. Environmental Protection Agency*
- The case dealt with the EPA's efforts under TSCA to regulate asbestos, one of the most dangerous carcinogens known.
- The EPA spent almost ten years reviewing and compiling evidence about the risk of asbestos in an effort to be thorough.
- Based on its analysis, the EPA decided that only a total ban of asbestos could avoid its known health risks.
- The EPA estimated that between 1988–2000, a ban would save at least 202 lives at a cost of $459 million—an acceptable cost, according to the EPA.
- The Fifth Circuit court reversed the EPA's ruling:
  - The EPA had compared risks and benefits of only two options: no regulation and a complete ban. A "middle way" set of regulations might have better balanced risks and benefits.
  - The court criticized the EPA's failure to quantify risks/benefits beyond 2000.
  - The court said the EPA should have examined potential risks of asbestos substitutes as well.
  - The court ruled that the EPA should have performed separate risk-benefit analyses for each product, not just all products in aggregate.
  - In effect, the court ruled that the EPA should have performed a perfect risk-benefit analysis.
    1. But this would have increased the difficulty of implementing TSCA and getting anything done at all.

- The case raises the question of the appropriate role of courts and administrative agencies in determining risk levels.
  - The EPA would seem to be in a better position than courts to do this; it is also more directly responsible to the public for its actions.

Suggested Discussion Questions
1. Was the EPA right in calling for a total ban of asbestos? Why or why not?
2. Who should determine risk levels—the EPA or the courts?

4.   Criticisms

Risk-benefit analysis has many critics.
- Some charge that this type of analysis slows down government regulation, making it unlikely that necessary action will occur (e.g., the *Corrosion Proof Fittings* case).
- Critics also sometimes worry that the government can too easily "cook the books" under the guise of scientific risk assessment. Underlying an agency's "scientific" conclusions may be several important policy decisions.
- Still other critics raise concerns about the morality of using economic efficiency to guide environmental policy.

Despite these concerns, risk-benefit analysis will still continue—the modern world is not risk-free, and reducing risks can be economically costly. As long as that is true, people will ask whether certain regulations are "worthwhile."

D.   Informational Approaches

Another way to deal with toxins is to provide the public with information about toxic exposure and allow public pressure and market factors to address the problem.

1.   The Toxic Release Inventory

Under the Emergency Planning and Community Right-to-Know Act of 1986 (EPCRA), the EPA maintains a list of about 600 hazardous substances.
- Any company that releases more than a certain amount of each substance in any calendar year must report releases to both the EPA and the state.
- The EPA then compiles data into a national toxic release inventory (TRI), which it makes public. This information is reported in the media and used by environmental groups to mobilize public awareness.

To avoid bad publicity, many companies work hard to reduce their releases rather than land a place on the TRI.

However, TRI is not perfect.
- Some companies reduce their emissions simply by changing reporting standards.

- Material sent for recycling is not counted as a TRI release, possibly skewing results.
- Companies must report only releases of toxins into the environment, not uses of toxins in their products.
- TRI covers only a fraction of known toxins and does not address releases by some major sources, such as farms.

Suggested Discussion Activity
1. Have students visit the EPA web site at http://www.epa.gov/tri/ to learn more about the toxic release inventory. There is a spot on the web site (http://www.epa.gov/tri/stakeholders/communities/index.htm) where you can type in your zip code to determine if there were any recent toxic chemical releases in your community.

2. *California's Proposition 65*

In 1986, California voters approved Proposition 65, requiring public disclosure of both toxic releases and toxic ingredients in consumer products.

Under Proposition 65, the state publishes a list of 750 chemicals known to cause cancer or reproductive toxicity.
- Businesses cannot discharge a listed chemical into water or on land if it would get into drinking water.
- They also cannot knowingly and intentionally expose someone to a listed substance without providing a "clear and reasonable" warning.

Businesses are exempt if the amount of the substance is "insignificant."
- However, the burden of proof falls on the business, not the government.

Proposition 65 also establishes a "bounty" provision.
- Whoever brings a lawsuit for violation receives 25 percent of any penalty imposed by the court.

Some people questioned whether consumers would pay attention to warning labels and signs.
- Warnings began popping up everywhere, making them commonplace and easy to ignore. Plus, the signs are very generic.
- However, Proposition 65 has resulted in significant reduction of toxic exposures. Example: Makers of Progresso tomatoes stopped using lead solder in their cans.
  o And, since manufacturers don't want to produce one version of a product just for California, changes they have implemented have benefited all Americans, not just Californians.

Suggested Discussion Question

1. Why do you think California voters approved Proposition 65? Do any other states have similar legislation? Why do you think Californians believed that this type of legislation was necessary?

PART II
Pollution Law

CHAPTER 8
Waste Management

I.   The Resource Conservation Recovery Act

American's lifestyle generates enormous amounts of waste.
- Every day, Americans generate the equivalent of 4.5 pounds of municipal solid waste for every man, woman, and child—an almost 70% increase from 1960.
- Only about 1% of household waste is considered a health hazard; most hazardous waste is generated by industrial facilities.

Why is waste such a problem?
- The so-called "landfill crisis": the perception that we are running out of places to dispose of waste.
    o From 1988–1999, almost 70% of our landfills closed.
    o However, it's not that there is a lack of space to dispose of waste; instead, NIMBY (not in my backyard) pressures make it hard for new landfills to be created.
- Waste means inefficiency—by disposing of so much, we need to extract more resources to replace what we discard.
- The biggest problem posed by waste is its health effects.
    o Drinking water can be contaminated by leachate from landfills.
    o Incinerators that burn waste create hazardous air pollutants.

Before the 1970s, there were few requirements for waste disposal.
- 1965's Solid Waste Disposal Act encouraged—but did not require—states to develop waste management programs.
- Many landfills were just holes in the ground where waste was dumped; when they got full, they were bulldozed, covered with topsoil, and turned into commercial developments.

Into this environment was crafted the Resource Conservation and Recovery Act (RCRA)—an amendment to the Solid Waste Disposal Act. RCRA has four goals:
- It creates definitions to determine the classes of wastes coming under its authority.
- It creates a tracking system for hazardous waste from its creation to disposal.
- It establishes handling standards for waste from creation to disposal.

- It provides authority for mandatory cleanup of polluted treatment, storage, and disposal facilities.

RCRA's key provisions deal with the disposal of solid waste (Subtitle D) and the treatment and disposal of hazardous waste (Subtitle C).
- However, many of the terms and meanings used in RCRA are counterintuitive and difficult to understand.

Suggested Discussion Question
1. Discuss waste disposal in your community. Where is the waste disposed of? How much waste is disposed annually?

A.   What Is It?

RCRA is an "all-or-nothing" proposition; either your waste is covered by the statute, or it is not. Therefore, the first questions to consider are: is the waste "solid," and is it solid "hazardous" waste?

1.   Solid Waste and Strategic Behavior

RCRA regulates only the disposal of "solid waste," which covers virtually every substance except uncontained gases. (This broad definition was born from the expectation that parties would simply add water to their waste and claim that it was no longer "solid.")

However, large amounts of waste are exempt:
- Some are exempt because they are regulated by other statutes.
- Municipal garbage is exempt because of its sheer size.
- Some wastes, such as irrigation flows, are exempt for political reasons (in this case, the farm lobby's influence).
- These exemptions encourage strategic behavior by the regulated community to try to avoid the most stringent regulations.

The RCRA covers only solid wastes that are waste products.
- Waste can also resemble products or raw materials. Example: Farmers commonly keep large vats of pesticides, which can be legally used under FIFRA even though runoffs enter waterways. But under RCRA, the same substances cannot be disposed of in landfills without special treatment—they are now considered "waste."
- Recycling poses a similar challenge.
    o Recycling often creates significant wastes itself.

American Mining Congress v. EPA I:
- In this case, the American Mining Congress argued that the wastes it produced during manufacturing should not be considered solid waste because they would later be used in other processes—not "discarded."
- The D.C. Circuit Court agreed with AMC's argument.
  o Afterward, RCRA's definition of solid waste seemed to depend as much on the owner's plans for the materials as on the nature of the materials.
  o This created an incentive not only for real recycling, but also for sham recycling—stating that you intended to reuse materials but simply storing them on-site indefinitely.

American Mining Congress v. EPA II:
- In this case, AMC argued that sludge stored in a surface impoundment (a holding pond) should not be considered RCRA solid waste because it was being held for potential reuse.
- The court decided that the recycling exemption only applies to wastes that are safely stored for immediate reuse (within 90 days) in an ongoing process (the same process). Otherwise, the materials are solid waste.

American Petroleum Institute v. EPA:
- American Petroleum Institute argued that the by-products of a manufacturing process should not be considered solid waste once they arrived at a reclamation facility for recycling.
- The court disagreed—the material remains solid waste under these circumstances because it has already become part of the waste disposal problem.

The greatest challenge in drafting regulations can be trying to fulfill the statute's intent while knowing that the regulated community will try to take advantage of any favorable treatment.

Suggested Discussion Questions
1. Does your community have a recycling program? Do students participate? Why or why not?
2. What wastes does recycling create?

2.   *Solid Hazardous Waste and Closing Loopholes*

RCRA distinguishes between two broad categories of covered wastes.
- Solid wastes are covered by Subtitle D.
- Solid and hazardous wastes are covered by Subtitle C. The definition of "hazardous" is fairly straightforward. RCRA identifies two categories:
  o *Listed wastes* are substances the EPA has identified as hazardous and listed in the Code of Federal Regulations.
  o *Characteristic wastes* are unlisted but have the characteristics of being hazardous (e.g., ignitable, corrosive, reactive, or toxic).

As emphasized previously, companies often try to avoid RCRA coverage. How can they attempt to avoid Subtitle C coverage?
- They could petition the EPA for delisting of a specific substance.
- They could try to modify the waste so it no longer has hazardous characteristics.

RCRA regulates treated wastes differently depending on whether they are listed or characteristic.
- If characteristic wastes are modified so that they no longer exhibit their hazardous characteristics, they are no longer covered by Section C.
- Listed wastes, though, are subject to two rules:
  o The mixture rule states that a mixture of a listed waste with another substance is still considered hazardous.
  o The derived-from rule states that wastes derived from the treatment of a hazardous waste also are considered hazardous.
  o A related contained-in policy holds that contaminated media (usually soil) becomes a hazardous waste.

RCRA's rules thus require strict treatment of many wastes that are much less hazardous than wastes that are not covered at all because of exemptions.

B.   Who Am I?

1.   Generators, Transporters, and TSDs

RCRA divides the world of actors into three categories: (1) generators, (2) transporters, and (3) treatment, storage, and disposal facilities (TSDs).
- RCRA follows the disposal of waste by creating a "cradle-to-grave" tracking system from the generators to the TSDs.
- When a generator produces a certain amount of hazardous waste, it must fill out a manifest sheet that accompanies the waste shipment each stage along the way to the TSD.
- This tracking system tries to eliminate the problem of unidentified wastes at contaminated sites.

Generators are subject to a number of requirements.
- They must determine if their waste is a listed or characteristic hazardous waste.
- They must store and label material properly, file various reports, and maintain scrupulous records about substances.

Transporters face fewer requirements than generators. They must, however, comply with EPA and Department of Transportation requirements for the transport of hazardous materials—including proper packaging, labeling, reporting, and so forth.

RCRA's requirements are the most stringent for TSDs.
- TSDs must obtain a permit from the EPA or an authorized state agency; this can take up to four years. The permit is good for ten years.

- TSDs must train personnel, keep proper records, monitor ground water, maintain security, and perform other operational functions.
- The technical standards required of TSDs are rigorous; for example, they require that landfills have two or more impermeable liners and a leachate collection system.
- TSDs must create a comprehensive plan for closure and must provide financial assurance (through insurance, for example) that they can pay for such closure, as well as any subsequent liability.

Amendments to RCRA in 1984 by the Hazardous and Solid Waste Amendments (HSWA) helped further assure that TSDs do not become Superfund cleanup sites.
- The EPA is allowed to authorize "corrective actions" forcing TSDs to clean up present or past contamination on their sites following the release of hazardous materials.
- To date there have been over 5,000 corrective actions ordered.

Suggested Discussion Activity
1. Have students search the Internet to find a list of Superfund cleanup sites. Are any of the sites located near your community?

2. The Land Ban and Regulatory Hammers

By the mid-1980s, Subtitle C's requirements had raised the cost of waste disposal, promoting the so-called "waste hierarchy": first reduce, then reuse, then recycle, then landfill.

But how to minimize landfill and the fear of groundwater contamination?
- HSWA greatly restricted the land disposal of wastes; it is allowed only if there will be "no migration" of hazardous constituents from the landfill.
- But Congress created an exception for wastes that had been treated to reduce toxicity.
- The "land ban" effectively prohibits only the disposal of untreated hazardous waste.
- The "hammer" provision shifts the burden of regulatory delay from the agency to industry by providing that if pretreatment regulations were not issued for a particular waste by a particular date, there would be no land-based disposal of that waste *at all*.

How should pre-treatment standards for hazardous waste be determined? Congress did not clearly answer, so the EPA was faced with two different approaches:
- The best available technology approach—which could overtreat the waste to levels far below any proven health risk.
- The risk assessment approach—which treats waste to a level with acceptable health risks.

- The EPA's final decision to go with a technology-based standard was upheld in *Hazardous Waste Treatment Council v. EPA*.
  - The EPA commenced with a hybrid policy, requiring pre-treatment by the best available technology but only to a degree needed to move below maximum concentration of hazardous materials.
  - Under pressure from Congress and environmentalists, who argued that "no migration" meant just that, the EPA later moved to a pure technological approach.

Going with a pure technological approach angered economists, though.
- The Office of Management and Budget estimated that the cost of the land ban was about $4 billion for each life saved. But did OMB reach this conclusion carefully?
- Despite scientific evidence, the public rates groundwater contamination high on its list of environmental concerns.

Media shifting is another problem: Following the land ban, the amount of waste sent to landfills decreased but the amount sent to incinerators increased. The waste simply shifted form, it did not just go away.

Suggested Discussion Question
1. Was the cost of the land ban worth the benefits derived from it?

C.   *Subtitle D*

State and local governments are largely responsible for the regulation of solid non-hazardous waste. (In 2007, such waste added up to 254.1 million tons.)
- Yet municipal waste still contains some hazardous materials (e.g., nickel-cadmium batteries), even though it is exempt from Subtitle C regulations.
- Subtitle D requires states to create plans to responsibly manage these wastes.
- The EPA also has created regulations for states and communities to follow. These set minimum standards, and states are free to regulate landfills more strictly as needed.

Suggested Discussion Question
1. What other potentially hazardous materials besides batteries wind up in our landfills? How can people become educated about the proper disposal of these materials?

D.   *The Challenge of Pollution Prevention*

It is important to note what RCRA does not cover.
- The environmental impacts of raw material inputs and product outputs of a typical manufacturing process are regulated, if at all, by other statutes such as TSCA and FIFRA. OSHA regulates occupational exposure to contaminants during manufacturing.

- RCRA covers only the waste stream.

Environmental law generally treats factories as giant "black boxes," kicking in only when the waste leaves the facility.
- This "end-of-pipe" approach has successfully improved air and water quality.
- But has it been efficient? It would seem, in fact, to favor *pollution control* strategies, in which waste disposal simply becomes a cost of doing business.
- Would it not be better for companies to use *pollution prevention* strategies to produce less waste in the first place?
    o Pollution prevention focuses on good housekeeping, waste audits, and improved production processes.

RCRA does little to promote pollution prevention. By dealing only with the *results* of the production process, RCRA misses the most important waste disposal issue of all—waste reduction at the *source*.

Suggested Discussion Activity
1. Divide the class into two groups and have them debate the use of pollution control versus pollution prevention.

II.   The Basel Convention

Wastes generated in both developed and developing countries have increased greatly in recent decades.
- The UN Environment Program estimates that generation of hazardous waste has increased by more than 60 times since the end of World War II.
- Shipment of this waste to developing countries has been common until recently; environment and health concerns, however, have led the international community to develop a way to govern this trade.

Only about 4% of hazardous wastes generated by OECD countries are shipped across international borders. However, the overall volume is very high.
- The export of recyclable or recoverable materials is big business, generating billions of dollars every year. Most waste shipped overseas is, in fact, shipped not for final disposal but for recovery.
    o But how to distinguish between shipments meant for legitimate recycling and unsafe disposal?
- Another factor driving transboundary shipments of waste is cost. It is often much cheaper to import waste to a developing country—partly because these countries typically do not stringently or effectively regulate waste imports.
    o There have been several environmental tragedies associated with the illegal or improper shipment of hazardous waste to developing countries (e.g., *Khian Sea* and Koko, Nigeria incidents).
    o Developing countries have denounced the cheap dumping of waste in their countries as "toxic colonialism."

Because of the foregoing, in 1989 the Basel Convention on the Control of Transboundary Movements of Hazardous Wastes and their Disposal was adopted by 116 countries.
- The Basel Convention establishes a global notification and consent system for the transboundary shipment of wastes among parties.
  - o Parties may not initiate the export of wastes without written (a) consent of the importing country, (b) consent of any transit countries, and (c) confirmation from the importing country of a written contract between the exporter and the disposer affirming the environmentally responsible disposal of the waste.
- Basel defines wastes as "substances or objects which are disposed of or are intended to be disposed of." The same prior consent is required for wastes intended for recycling/reclamation as for disposal, to avoid "sham recycling" problems discussed previously.
- Parties to Basel may not trade wastes if either the exporting or importing country thinks the wastes will not be managed responsibly.
- Basel relies on trade-related measures to encourage states to become parties. It prohibits parties from trading wastes with non-parties and further commits parties to honor import bans adopted by other parties.
  - o However, it does allow imports/exports of covered wastes between parties and non-parties if they are subject to another appropriate, bilateral, multilateral, or regional agreement.

Obviously, Basel has not banned the waste trade; it has rather created a global prior informed consent regime. There are two good reasons for this:
- First, it would be unwise to kill the waste trade because many developing countries use materials recovered from waste, providing many jobs and revenue.
- Second, a ban would be paternalistic by denying developing countries to decide for themselves whether or not to accept the risks associated with importing wastes.
- A strong counter argument in favor of a trade ban is that it should not be allowed simply because developing countries can use the money. After all, for example, governments could make money by permitting slavery, yet few would justify this action. Waste trade is simply exploitation of the poor by the wealthy and powerful.

In reaction against Basel's failure to ban the waste trade, some nations have created multilateral treaties regulating it.
- The 51 member states of the Organization for African Unity adopted the Bamako Convention on the Ban of Import Into Africa and the Control of Transboundary Movement and Management of Hazardous Wastes Within Africa.
  - o Bamako requires all parties to prohibit the import of waste from outside Africa.
- Going further, the former European colonies in Africa, the Caribbean, and the Pacific banned the direct/indirect export of any hazardous or radioactive waste from European Union states (the Lomé IV Convention).

- Some NGOs such as Greenpeace have also been working toward a complete trade ban between parties/non-parties of the Organization for Economic Cooperation and Development (OECD).
  - In 1995, parties adopted an amendment (the Basel Ban) that would prohibit hazardous waste shipments from OECD or EU parties to non-OECD/EU countries.

The United States, Haiti, and Afghanistan are the only three countries that have signed but not ratified the Basel Convention.

Suggested Discussion Question and Activity
1. Divide the class into two groups and have them debate whether the waste trade should be banned. One group supports waste trade; the other group thinks it should be banned.
2. Why hasn't the United States ratified the Basel Convention?

III. The Comprehensive Emergency Response, Compensation and Liability Act

The most controversial environmental law has probably been the Comprehensive Emergency Response, Compensation and Liability Act (CERCLA, aka Superfund).
- While RCRA addresses the issue of current waste disposal, CERCLA responds to problems from prior waste disposal practices and imposes liability to ensure that contaminated sites are cleaned up.
- The imposition of liability has sparked criticism of CERCLA's fairness and cost effectiveness.

The Love Canal incident was the main spark behind the drafting of CERCLA.
- In the 1960s and 1970s, a number of Love Canal, NY, residents began complaining of a wide variety of health problems—including cancer, birth defects, and miscarriages.
- Soil samples in 1978 revealed high levels of chemical contaminants in the soil and air.
- Further study revealed that much of Love Canal had been built atop an old landfill containing over 21,000 tons of chemical waste, which had broken through its clay liner and seeped into soil and even people's basements.
- President Carter declared a State of Emergency, finding new homes for 239 families; federal funding was subsequently provided for the permanent relocation of all 900 Love Canal families.

Love Canal revealed that no law dealt with hazardous wastes that had been buried years ago. How many potential Love Canals were out there? To address the problem adequately, four basic challenges had to be dealt with in any legislation:

- How to identify and prioritize the problem sites.
- Who should perform the cleanup?
- Who should pay for the cleanup?
- How clean is clean?

To adequately understand CERCLA, one needs to consider the options Congress did *not* choose; it is telling that *no* country has subsequently followed the approach set out in CERCLA.

Finally, one must understand a bit about the circumstances surrounding CERCLA's passage.
- It was passed by Congress and signed into law during the "lame duck" session between Carter's electoral defeat and Reagan's taking office.
- Because it was put together quickly, the law is not well drafted.
- The Reagan administration was opposed to CERCLA and blocked its implementation to the extent that the reputation of the EPA was damaged.

Suggested Discussion Activity
1. Have students research and write a brief report on the Love Canal incident.

A.   *The Cleanup Process*

CERCLA doesn't require anyone to do anything . . . other than notify the EPA of any known releases of a reportable quantity of hazardous waste. The rest of the statute creates a cleanup process:
- It gives the government power to require cleanup.
- It gives government and private parties the authority to recover cleanup costs.

1.   Listing and Prioritization of Sites

To determine which sites should be cleaned up first, the EPA created a National Priority List (NPL) of the most seriously contaminated sites.

Sites are ranked according to their score based on the Hazard Rating System, which accounts for a site's toxicity, closeness to local population, and so forth.

By the end of 2008, the EPA had conducted final assessments of over 40,000 sites; over 1,200 had been listed between 1985–2009.

Suggested Discussion Activity
1. Have students visit the EPA web site and find the national priority list for your state. Where are those sites located? Are any located near your community?

2.   Responses

CERCLA takes effect whenever there has been a "release" or a "substantial threat of release" of a "hazardous substance" into the environment from a "facility."
- "Release" has been broadly defined to encompass almost any event where a hazardous substance left its container.
- A "substantial threat of release" covers substances still contained in corroding tanks or abandoned drums.
- "Hazardous substances" have been broadly defined to include almost anything considered hazardous under other pollution statutes as well as any other substances that the EPA determines may be hazardous.
- A "facility" is virtually any type of place or structure.

Once the threat of release of a hazardous substance from a facility has been established, CERCLA authorizes two types of cleanups:
- A "removal action" is short term; it is intended to alleviate immediate dangers to the public health.
- A "remediation" is a longer-term action that seeks to provide—as much as is possible—a permanent remedy to the problem.
- All cleanups must follow the requirements set out in the National Contingency Plan (NCP), including provisions for extensive remedial investigations and feasibility studies (RI/FS).

B.   Compensation for Response Actions

Three types of response actions are allowable under CERCLA—all driven by the notion that the taxpayer should not be responsible for paying for cleanup costs.
- The EPA can perform the cleanup itself and sue the potentially responsible parties (PRPs) later.
  - o To pay for cleanup, the EPA draws from the "Superfund," a sum funded primarily by chemical and petroleum taxes.
  - o Superfund was quickly drawn down because PRPs more often sued the EPA than paid for cleanup.
- Another option is for the EPA to order PRPs to perform the cleanup.
  - o Many suits have been filed by entities ordered to perform cleanups, on the grounds that they are not PRPs.
- A third form of compensation applies to private parties that have cleaned up a site; these parties can sue other PRPs to recover costs.

CERCLA also authorizes federal and state governments and Indian tribes to sue for "natural resource damages" to pay for both the restoration and cost of damaged resources. There is no private right of action to do so.

Suggested Discussion Question
1. Should taxpayers pay for part of the cleanup costs? Why or why not?

1.   Potentially Responsible Parties (PRPs)

CERCLA establishes four broad categories of PRPs:
- Current owners and operators of a facility (even if they were not owners/operators when disposal occurred).
- Prior owners or operators at the time of disposal.
- Arrangers of disposal or treatment (aka "generators").
- Transporters (if they played a major role in selecting the facility).

2.   Liability Standards

The categories of PRPs delineate who potentially might pay, while CERCLA's most controversial provisions concern liability—who actually does pay.
- CERCLA refers to Section 311 of the Clean Water Act's oil spill program, which refers to common law principles, which in turn courts have interpreted to be the standard of strict, joint, and several liability.
- The strict liability provision does away with the need for proof of negligence, intent, or harm.
- The joint and several provision means that a single party could be liable for all the costs even if 20 other parties were also PRPs.

A strict, joint, and several liability standard creates significant fairness concerns.
- Example: A PRP who pays for the government's cleanup costs can bring a contribution action against other PRPs—but not all PRPs may be available toward the cleanup act (some may have gone bankrupt, for instance).
  - As a result, current PRPs must shoulder the burden of paying for these "orphan shares."
- Also, by making all PRPs potentially responsible for the cleanup, there is an incentive for PRPs to implicate as many other PRPs as possible. The high cost of locating PRPs has diverted lots of money from actual cleanups.
- Finally, a strict, joint, and several liability policy standard can easily turn into a search for PRPs with "deep pockets," even if they have minor actual responsibility.

The biggest concern raised by the retroactive liability standards and broad categories of PRPs is that of fairness.
- Are all PRPs really equally liable? Can they fairly be held liable for actions taken years ago, even if they were legal at the time?
- The traditional explanation has been that these PRPs benefited from the low costs associated with waste disposal practices in the past and should bear the cleanup costs now when they arise.

C.   Defenses

The primary ways for a PRP to escape liability are discussed below.

1.   Acts of God, War, or a Third Party

CERCLA exempts releases caused by an "act of God," an "act of war," or an act of a third party.

- Act of God and war defenses have rarely been successful because most disasters can actually be anticipated; only exceedingly rare and unforeseen circumstances apply.
- Exemptions can also be granted if the release was caused by the act or omission of a third party and the PRP exercised due care.
    o This defense does not apply, though, if there is any direct or indirect relationship between the defendant and the party responsible for the release.

Suggested Discussion Question
1. Should PRPs be held liable in cases of catastrophe, such as Hurricane Katrina?

2.   Divisibility

Joint and several liability can be avoided if a PRP can show its waste is divisible.

- This would appear to be easy. Example: Your facility sends 100 barrels of waste to a site that accepted 1,000 barrels. You agree to help fund the cleanup because you contributed, but shouldn't your contribution be limited to 10% of the costs— since you contributed only 10% of the barrels?
- Actually, no. If the waste has escaped, then it has mixed with other waste in the site. Because of diffusion in the soil, you need to remove all the waste in order to remove the part you are responsible for.
- The burden falls on the PRP to demonstrate that its harm is divisible.

In the past, most courts and the EPA have imposed joint and several liability on PRPs, with divisibility defenses having little success.

- However, in *Burlington Northern & Santa Fe Railway v. United States*, the U.S. Supreme Court held in 2009 that, in spite of the fact that a contamination event may cause a single harm, such harm may still be divisible if the defendant demonstrates a rational basis for apportionment.
- In such cases, courts may apportion the costs among the named defendants based on the sufficiency of evidence.

3.   Small Contributors

If the EPA determines that a PRP contributed a minimal amount of hazardous waste to a site, compared with other PRPs, CERCLA allows the EPA to reach an early "de minimus" settlement with the PRP, with complete absolution from additional or future liability, in return for payment of a premium over what would otherwise be a fair share.

Further, if a PRP can show that it contributed less than 110 gallons of liquid or less than 200 pounds of solid material prior to April 2001, it can qualify for a "de micromis" exemption.

Similar exemptions have been created for small businesses, homeowners, and the like.

4.   Municipalities

Towns' and cities' landfills have often received hazardous wastes, but the EPA has long had a policy of not going after municipalities for cost recovery actions. However, PRPs can and do sue municipalities for private contribution.

Suggested Discussion Question
   1.   Why doesn't the EPA hold municipalities responsible for hazardous waste?

5.   Lenders

CERCLA excludes owners and operators from liability if they hold an "indicia of ownership" in a property primarily as a security interest.

If a bank is actively involved in the property's management, or if it has taken outright ownership, though, it would become a PRP (see *United States v. Fleet Factors Corp.*).

Some courts assigned broad liability in such cases; others were much narrower. Which policy is better?
   - Arguments in favor of making banks liable:
     - They can act as effective gatekeepers, ensuring that borrowers be environmentally responsible with their waste disposal.
     - If banks are not held liable, where is the incentive for them to ensure the waste on the property is properly taken care of?
     - Finally, banks have plenty of money to spend on cleanup efforts.
   - Arguments against unlimited liability:
     - Lenders have, in fact, never served as *effective* gatekeepers: it's not their area of expertise.
   - Making banks liable could dry up credit; if companies that handle hazardous waste cannot get financing, they will be more likely to operate cheaply and be unable to fix problems.

To solve the debate, in 1996 Congress passed the Asset Conservation, Lender Liability, and Deposit Insurance Protection Act.
   - Banks can foreclose on property "if the person seeks to sell . . . or otherwise divest . . . the vessel or facility . . . at the earliest practicable, commercially reasonable time, on commercially reasonable terms, taking into account market conditions and legal and regulatory requirements. . ."
   - To lose the exemption, a bank must (a) be a decision maker regarding environmental compliance or (b) exercise overall management control.

Suggested Discussion Activity
1. Divide the class into two groups and have them debate holding lenders liable for waste cleanup. One group will argue in favor of making banks liable; the other will argue against unlimited liability.

6.   Innocent Landowners

CERCLA originally imposed liability on all current owners of contaminated property. In response to complaints of unfairness, in the 1986 SARA amendments Congress extended the third-party defense to "innocent landowners."

- To qualify, property owners must have undertaken "all appropriate inquiry" before purchasing the property and have no real knowledge of the hazards.
- The "all appropriate inquiry" provision has been raised to a high standard to ensure that owners cannot avoid liability just by asking a few questions about the property.
- New Jersey's Environmental Cleanup Responsibility Act (ECRA) requires owners to demonstrate that a property is not contaminated by hazardous materials before transferring ownership to another party.

7.   Settlement Strategies

PRPs have few defenses when faced with cost recovery or contribution action.
- However, the *Burlington Northern* case discussed previously may shift this balance.

Despite the *Burlington Northern* decision, the strict liability imposed on PRPs forces potential PRPs to become more vigilant. If a party realizes that the actions of other parties could result in it becoming a PRP, it will take a closer look at its own—as well as the other parties'—actions. Formerly remote players are forced to act as surrogate regulators.

D.   Brownfields

A brownfield is an abandoned, idle, or underused industrial and/or commercial facility where expansion or redevelopment is complicated by real or perceived environmental contamination.

In many American cities, brownfields dot the urban landscape.
- Developers are wary of purchasing them for fear that they will become PRPs if the sites are later found to be contaminated.
- Banks are wary of financing development of brownfields even if someone is willing to do it.
- As a result, brownfields sit vacant while developers seek suburban sites ("greenfields") that are likely to be cleaner.
  - This trend increases urban sprawl, removes economic opportunity from the cities, and leaves urban areas derelict.

Community groups often argue about the proper approach to the brownfields problem.
- Leaving urban sites undeveloped benefits no one; developing such sites would create jobs and strengthen the community.
- Others argue that this is a case of environmental injustice: Why should these sites not be cleaned? Development on contaminated land is worse than no development at all.

Federal and state governments have been working hard to reduce brownfield problems.
- Examples: To spur development, the Department of Housing and Urban Development and the EPA have offered grants, and tax breaks are also available. In 2009 alone, for example, over $37 million in grants were approved by the EPA for brownfields development.
- In addition, 47 states plus the District of Columbia and Puerto Rico provide for voluntary cleanup programs that act as a shield from enforcement actions.

Suggested Discussion Activity
1. Have students visit the EPA's web site to learn more about brownfields. Discuss findings in class.

E.   How Clean Is Clean?

Environmental justice issues have arisen over the proper level of remediation at contaminated sites. Should all sites be equally clean after remediation? What role should costs play in the equation?

CERCLA never resolved the issue of "how clean is clean"; much discretion has been left to the EPA. The 1986 SARA amendments require the EPA to consider a number of factors, such as human health and the environment, in determining "how clean is clean."
- Additionally, the level of cleanup must satisfy so-called ARARs (Applicable, Relevant and Appropriate Requirements).

What would be a better solution?
- Uniform national goals for residual contamination would ensure equitable cleanups but could be economically inefficient.
- Cleanup standards could be tailored to local conditions by requiring cleanup to background levels; but this takes no account of risk or cost.
- A uniform level of risk could be set; each site might seek to reduce risk from contamination to, say, 1 death in 1 million.
- One could rely on a site classification approach that assumes standards could differ from site to site; standards for a playground would be greater than for a commercial site.

Also crucial is the procedural issue of *who* should decide "how clean is clean."
- Local communities will want the greatest level of cleanup possible; PRPs will seek to keep costs down.

- Fundamentally, this is a political question pitting efficiency and fairness against one another.

Suggested Discussion Question
1. Which is the better solution for determining the level of cleanup needed? Who should decide the standards?

F.   *Superfund Reform*

Superfund has been the victim of high expectations and low performance.
- CERCLA has been very expensive, and as much as 40% of the money is spent on lawsuits and studies rather than cleanups.

Administration of the program seems to have become more efficient in recent years, with less litigation and more pre-settlement negotiation. And there have been some real successes:
- Over 6,400 removal actions have taken place at hazardous waste sites.
- By July of 2009, work had been completed at 1,065 NPL sites, and was underway at 423 sites.
- PRPs have paid for about 70% of the cleanup costs, amounting to over $16 billion.
- EPA has reached over 430 de minimis settlements with more than 21,000 small waste contributors.
- About $8 of private response costs have been spent for every $1 of public funds spent on enforcement.

Still, most people believe Superfund could be improved—either in terms of fairness or cost-effectiveness.
- Since 2003, its funding has come from general revenues appropriated by Congress and litigation awards from PRPs.
- Other funding reforms have ranged from eliminating liability-based funding for disposal prior to 1986 and more generous de minimis provisions, to greater protection of municipalities and subsequent land purchasers.
    - But all of these proposals would let some parties off the hook, which is why CERCLA has remained largely unchanged.
    - Once the decision is made that taxpayers will not pay for cleanups, CERCLA reform becomes a zero sum game. Any reform that lessens the liability of some PRPs will increase it for others.

Despite all of its criticisms and problems, one must keep in mind the benefits of avoided Love Canals as well.

Suggested Discussion Question

1. List some of the Superfund's achievements and the improvements that could still be made to it.

PART III
Trade

————

CHAPTER 9
Trade and Environment

In the late 1980s, a majority of states began requiring or urging newspapers to use recycled content in their newsprint. But environmentalists were not the ones pushing this; America's pulp and paper producers were.

Why? Trade.

- The recycling requirements resulted in Canadian pulp and paper firms importing waste paper from the U.S., recycling it, then shipping it back to the U.S. This increased U.S. pulp and paper companies' market share.

What questions are involved in the trade and environment debate?

- Are American lawmakers more interested in protecting the environment, or U.S. companies?
- Who should decide the law's motivation?
- How should it be decided?
- What should happen if the law is deemed to be primarily protectionist?

Conflicts between free trade and environmental protection are not always international. There are also interstate tensions between free commerce and environmental protection.

However, the media tends to focus on international trade and environment conflicts, largely because of the huge increase in international economic activity.

I.   The Trade Debate

There would seem to be strong arguments in favor of increased international trade and capitals flow.

- Trade flows increase wealth.
  - o Economic growth is the first step toward alleviating poverty.
    1. The World Bank reports that almost half of the world's population lives on less than $2.50/day; about one-fifth live on less than $1.25/day.
  - o Rising incomes will produce more resources for pollution control and cleanup (e.g., demand for a cleaner environment is "income-elastic").
- Free trade can promote more efficient use of resources. Liberalized trade encourages nations to concentrate on their production of goods and services.

- o The theory of comparative advantage says that each country will specialize in and export goods it produces more efficiently relative to other nations.
  - o Economies of scale allow goods to be produced more economically when the scale of their production is increased.
  - o International competition forces companies to innovate, upgrade, and anticipate demand—making them more efficient and allowing them to offer consumers more products at lower prices.
- There are political benefits to international trade also; countries that are tied economically are less likely to wage war against each other.
  - o This was a key motivation for the creation of the European Community after World War II.
  - o The same geopolitical motivation underpinned the founding of the General Agreement on Tariffs and Trade (GATT) also.
  - o Conflicts between former enemies such as France and Germany and Japan and the U.S. have been resolved peacefully over the past 50 years, partly because of strong economic ties between the nations.

All of the above benefits notwithstanding, international trade has plenty of critics.
- Anti-growth/anti-globalization critics argue that current models of development have harmed the environment, so expanding trade will simply result in further environmental devastation.
  - o Increasing per capita income does not automatically lead to environmental improvement everywhere; it often leads to greater consumption and excess.
  - o Also, the distribution of wealth brought about by increased international trade is not equitable; the rich get richer, and the poor fall further behind.
- Liberalized trade may also threaten a country's ability to choose worthwhile domestic goals, such as high levels of environmental protection, food security, and so forth.
- Countries that choose high levels of environmental protection may suffer if industries leave for other nations with less stringent standards. This could ultimately result in degraded, not improved, environmental standards worldwide.

Suggested Discussion Question and Activity
1. What other types of international environmental trade can you think of besides recycling?
2. Divide the class into two groups and have them debate the international environmental trade issue. One group supports environmental trade; the other group is against it.

II.   The GATT and WTO

After World War II, the international community established three economic institutions: the World Bank, the International Monetary Fund, and the General Agreement on Tariffs and Trade (GATT).

- Originally intended to be a component of the larger International Trade Organization (ITO), GATT focused mainly on tariff reduction. It came into force in 1948.
- Subsequent ITO negotiations were abandoned, though, when it became obvious that the U.S. Congress would not ratify GATT.
- GATT subsequently evolved as an institution through a series of multilateral negotiating "rounds," such as the Uruguay Round that established the World Trade Organization (WTO), the successor to the ITO.
  - The WTO forms the legal and institutional framework for the multilateral trading system, proving a forum for implementing GATT.

GATT's objective is to reduce trade barriers among member states and to ensure that goods and services are not discriminated against based on their country of origin.

- The underlying diplomatic principle of GATT is that increased trade will create political bonds between nations, thus enhancing international security.
- GATT's provisions (called "disciplines") are almost entirely negative, taking into account the domestic realities of protectionism. Four are of particular interest:
  - Article I creates "most favored nation" (MFN) status, prevents members from "playing favorites" and discriminating between "like products" from other GATT members.
  - Article III establishes the "national treatment" obligation, preventing members from discriminating against other members' imports in favor of their own (domestic) like products.
    1. Articles I and III play out in the setting of tariff levels imposed on imports.
  - Article XI forbids quotas that limit the quantity of imports permitted.
  - Article XX provides for environmental exceptions to the requirements of Articles I, III, and XI (although the word "environment" is nowhere to be found in the text of GATT).

There are no private rights of action under the WTO's dispute settlement system; only member state governments may challenge other nations' laws or practices.

- Initially, disputing parties are asked to enter consultations to arrive at an agreeable solution.
- If this fails, the WTO Dispute Settlement Body establishes a panel to hear the dispute.
- After the panel rules, the losing party may appeal to an Appellate Body for review of issues of law. If the repeal is unsuccessful, the losing party may:
  - Remedy the offending measure, thus closing the matter.

- o Keep the offending measure in place, in which case the injured party may raise "countervailing tariffs" against imported products from the losing nation equal in value to the damage it is suffering by the offending trade measure.
- Damages are awarded from the time the decision was handed down.
  - o This results in the offending country "paying its way" until it comes into compliance.

The power of dispute panels to order effective sanctions against offending practices makes the WTO the envy of other international agreements.
- However, the panelist's trade backgrounds concern some environmentalists, who claim that they often do not understand environmental issues at hand.
- Environmentalists have also pressed the WTO to accept amicus curiae (friend of the court) briefs from public interest non-governmental organizations.
- Unlike most other international organizations, non-governmental organizations are not allowed to observe or participate in WTO meetings.

Suggested Discussion Activity
1. Have students choose either the WTO or GATT as the topic of a brief paper.

A.   *Like Products and PPMs*

The so-called "Tuna/Dolphin Case" was one of the first in the field of trade and environment.
- Bottlenose dolphins swim above schools of yellowfin tuna in the Eastern Tropical Pacific. This results in hundreds of thousands of dolphins being killed during tuna harvests.
- U.S. environmentalists and animal rights activists successfully convinced Congress to amend the Marine Mammal Protection Act to effectively require other countries to use "dolphin-friendly" nets when harvesting tuna.
  - o If the country could not prove the use of such nets, the amendment required the U.S. Secretary of Commerce to ban the imports of their tuna products.
  - o Tuna imports from a number of countries, including Mexico, were banned for this reason.

Mexico argued that the U.S. ban violated Articles I, III, and XI of GATT because its tuna was the same as U.S. tuna.
- The U.S. answered that these are not "like" products because "dolphin-friendly" tuna was not the same as Mexican tuna.
- Put another way, the U.S. ban was based as much on the process and production methods (PPMs) and their environmental impact as on the product itself.

The GATT panel found in favor of Mexico, shocking environmental groups worldwide.
- PPMs could not be the basis of a trade restriction, the panel found; "likeness" should be determined by a product's *physical* characteristics only.

- Article XX also did not apply in this case, since a country could not suspend trade rules for environmental harm occurring outside its borders.
- Though Mexico eventually dropped the case due to political concerns involving the North American Free Trade Agreement, the decision clearly represented the opinion of the trade community: one country did not have the right to impose its environmental ethics on another.
- The decision was also supported by developing countries, whose lower environmental standards give them some cost advantages and access to export markets.
    o American calls to ban products made with child labor is another example, such countries believe, where PPMs may be used as pretexts for protectionist measures.

The U.S. environmental community reacted strongly.
- They complained that the GATT panel had deliberately excluded environmental issues from the decision.
- The decision frustrated attempts to protect international resources.
- Was there any way for countries to use trade restrictions to protect the environment outside their jurisdictions?

Clarifying the PPM issue has been one of the key challenges in the trade and environment debate.
- Environmentalists argue that existing rules provide little guidance to policy makers.
    o Disallowing countries to distinguish between goods based on their environmental impact gives countries with lax environmental standards a competitive advantage.
    o It also forces importing countries to import and consume unsustainably produced goods.
- Trade theorists respond that different countries should be allowed to set their own environmental standards.
    o Different preferences for environmental quality are a valid source of comparative advantages.
    o Allowing countries to distinguish between goods based on their environmental impact will ultimately lead to protectionism.

Perhaps a better way to deal with different PPMs is to reduce differences between nations' environmental standards. There would then be less scope for international disputes to arise.

Another example is the *Shrimp-Turtle* decision, in which the U.S. banned the import of shrimp harvested with equipment that killed endangered sea turtles.
- The WTO Appellate Body ruled against the ban, in part because the U.S. had not negotiated adequately with affected states prior to banning the imports.

Subsequent cases have weakened the Tuna/Dolphin cases' stark holdings.

- Example: The WTO's Appellate Body has taken a more nuanced approach to the "like products" analysis, providing room for non-trade concerns and moving away from a narrow focus on a product's physical characteristics.
- The *Shrimp-Turtle* decision suggests that PPM-based measures may sometimes be justified under Article XX(g).
- Nonetheless, the only way a government can be confident that its environmental protection measures will not violate the GATT is if (1) the trade restrictions focus on the products themselves rather than how they were produced or harvested, (2) the harm is local, and (3) the measure is not unilaterally imposed.

In respect to international trade, U.S. environmental laws fall into three categories:
- Most will be unaffected by international trade rules because they have no major trade implications.
- Some are likely to be unaffected by GATT disciplines, but may have some trade implications.
- A small group of laws are based neither on local harms nor international consensus.
    - They are potential problems because they reflect value judgments.
    - Once value judgments can justify a trade barrier, one can provide a reason for any kind of protectionism.
    - Given the settlement dispute process, though, this may not be all bad.
        1. The international trade system allows us to use trade sanctions to remedy environmental harms we deem important, as long as we are willing to pay for our beliefs.

Suggested Discussion Questions and Activity
1. Do you think the U.S. should be able to impose its environmental ethics on other countries with which it trades? Why or why not?
2. Should GATT cover environmental concerns? Explain your reasoning.
3. Divide the class into two groups and have them debate the PPM issue. One group will represent the environmentalists; the other group will represent the trade theorists.

B.   Multilateral Environmental Agreements

The relationship between multilateral environmental agreements (MEAs) and GATT has been hotly debated.
- A number of MEAs rely on trade measures to protect the environment, sanction noncompliance by parties, or encourage nonparties to join.
- However, if a party and non-party to Basel or the Montreal Protocol are both GATT member states, such restrictions could violate Articles I and XI.

The Tuna/Dolphin decision described previously caused concern among environmentalists, who feared that several MEAs could be found in violation of GATT.
- If a WTO agreement conflicts with an MEA, which should take priority?

- o International law says that the more recent agreement wins, but is GATT considered a 1947 treaty or a 1995 treaty (revised during the Uruguay Round)?
- o Some believe that the WTO is an inappropriate forum to judge MEAs in any case.
- o Others suggest that the WTO should create a "safe harbor" to exempt trade provisions in MEAs.
- o In any event, there have been no challenges to date, and there are unlikely to be many—MEAs simply have so many parties.

III. The North American Free Trade Agreement (NAFTA)

In December 1992, the U.S., Canada, and Mexico concluded the North American Free Trade Agreement (NAFTA).
- NAFTA reduces tariffs and other trade barriers.
- It integrates the markets of the three countries into a single $8.6 trillion free trade area with annual trade flows of more than $600 billion (in 1992 figures).
- It has provisions that protect domestic health and environmental regulations from the downward pressures caused by free trade.

The NAFTA parties also concluded an Environmental Side Agreement, called the North American Agreement on Environmental Cooperation.
- Goals are environmental cooperation, greater citizen participation in environmental affairs, and better enforcement of environmental laws.

Original parties designed NAFTA with a view to eventually developing a Free Trade Agreement for the Americas, involving 34 nations in the Western hemisphere.
- MERCOSUR is a NAFTA counterpart involving five South American countries and four associate members.

Initial drafts of NAFTA included no environmental provisions.
- After labor and environmental groups protested, George H. W. Bush revised NAFTA to include some environmental protections.
- Environmentalists were concerned that different levels of environmental protection in the three countries would either prevent the strengthening of environmental laws or induce industry flight.
- As evidence, they pointed to the Maquiladora zone—a 60-mile wide free trade zone along the U.S.-Mexico border.
  - o Maquiladoras are factories owned jointly by U.S. and Mexican corporations and operated on the Mexican side of the U.S.-Mexico border.
  - o Since the establishment of the Maquiladora program in 1965, thousands of factories have opened along the border.
  - o Before NAFTA, Mexico had neither the money nor the political will to enforce its environmental laws, allowing the Maquiladoras to go virtually unregulated.

Suggested Discussion Question
1. Do you think NAFTA should include more environmental provisions? Why or why not?

A.   Environmental Provisions

NAFTA contains relatively few environmental provisions, but it does contain three important requirements:
- Article 1114.2 addresses the industry flight issue; it says that countries should not encourage investment and development by lowering environmental standards.
- Article 104 addresses potential conflict between trade measures in MEAs and NAFTA; generally, MEAs will win.
- NAFTA also addresses the potential role of sanitary and phytosanitary measures and other standards in acting as barriers to trade. Parties to the treaty can determine their own acceptable levels of protection; they can ban products if the risks are deemed to be too great.

B.   Environmental Side Agreement

Despite the foregoing provisions, NAFTA was strongly opposed by trade and environmental groups.
- Bill Clinton promised to add separate side agreements to address their concerns.
- The Environmental Side Agreement applies wherever parties believe environmental protection can be enhanced by cooperation.

Article 3 of the Side Agreement recognizes all parties' right to establish their own levels of domestic environmental protection, but they must enforce their laws to ensure that the standards are met.

The Side Agreement also created a way for the parties to cooperate: the North American Commission for Environmental Cooperation (CEC).
- The CEC consists of three organs: the Council, the Secretariat, and the Joint Public Advisory Committee.
- The Council is the CEC's political organ and governing body, composed of one cabinet-level representative from each member nation.
- The Joint Public Advisory Committee (JPAC) allows non-government organizations and individuals to influence the CEC's decisions.

The CEC has been crucial in publicizing and investigating environmental violations or non-enforcement.
- Article 13 of the NAAEC allows the Secretariat to prepare reports on most any environmental matter within the scope of the program, unless Council objects by a 2/3 vote.

- Per Article 13, the CEC may not report on whether or not a party has failed to properly enforce its environmental laws and regulations. But Article 14 allows citizens to file submissions to the Secretariat asserting such lack of enforcement.
  - If warranted, the CEC will identify specific instances of noncompliance.
  - Article 14 relies on research, data analysis, and publicity to encourage compliance with environmental law. (Note the contrasts to the WTO's approach.)
  - As of 2009, over 70 submissions had been made under Article 14.
- Article 22 of the Side Agreement states that if one party to the agreement believes that another party has consistently failed to enforce its environmental laws in relation to trade, it may request consultations to resolve the dispute.

C.   Chapter 11

The most controversial part of NAFTA has been Chapter 11's "investor-state" provision.
- Foreign investors have long feared "expropriation," the taking over of local operations. Example: Middle Eastern countries nationalized foreign oil company assets in the 1950s.
- Therefore, many foreign investor agreements provide for compensation of private parties in the event of expropriation.

Chapter 11 introduces two changes:
- The scope of offending actions is broadened.
  - Compensation is provided not only for direct expropriation, but for measures that are "tantamount to nationalization or expropriation."
- Private investors, not just the state, can sue a host state directly for a claim that an investor's right has been breached in the event of expropriation.
  - Positive: Removes diplomatic considerations from potential lawsuits.
  - Negative: Opens the floodgates to such suits, many of which may be warrantless.

Chapter 11's dispute settlement process is based on accepted international practice for commercial arbitration.
- A panel of three arbitrators is chosen from trade and investment law experts.
- Proceedings are generally kept secret.
- The challenged state bears the burden of proof to show that the restricted product or activity is unsafe.
- The panel's decision is binding on both parties, with limited appeal opportunities.

Ethyl Corp. v. Canada was the first case that highlighted the relationship between Chapter 11 and environmental protection.
- Ethyl Corporation sued the Canadian government for banning the import and inter-provincial transport of MMT, a gasoline additive that could pose a health risk.

- o Because the scientific data was inconclusive, MMT could not be prohibited under Canada's Environmental Protection Act—therefore, the only way to prevent its use was to ban its import/transport.
- Ethyl filed a notice of intent to arbitrate, claiming a number of damages including expropriation.
- Canada settled the case, paying Ethyl $13 million for costs and lost profits.

The *Metalclad* and *Methanex* cases were two other high-profile Chapter 11 cases.
- Chapter 11 challenges continue to raise concerns over chilling of environmental protection.
- The traditional takings exemption for so-called "police powers" does not seem to apply to Chapter 11.
- Finally, many companies have threatened to bring Chapter 11 challenges if certain substances are restricted or banned.
- Others dispute the foregoing concerns, pointing out that (a) government continues to function despite the threat of frivolous nuisance suits and (b) charges that NAFTA is undemocratic are unpersuasive given that our elected representatives signed and ratified it.

Suggested Discussion Activity
1. Have students go to the Public Citizen web site at http://www.citizen.org/trade/nafta/CH%5F%5F11/ and read about other Chapter 11 cases. Discuss some of these in class.

PART IV
Natural Resources

CHAPTER 10
Wetlands, Endangered Species, & the Public Trust

I. The Nation's Diminishing Resources

The U.S. is losing many of its natural resources.
- Nearly 60% of the nation outside Alaska has lost its native vegetation.
- More than half the nation's wetlands have disappeared—80% or more in some states.
- Thousands of America's waterways run dry some part of the year; others barely trickle.
- Loss of habitat has led to a decline in species.

Resources vital to America's economic well-being are included in this loss. Examples:
- The nation's farm and range soil has lost up to 15% of its natural mineral content due to erosion and poor agricultural management.
- In about 50% of the states, water users are pumping more groundwater from wells than nature is replenishing.
- About 1/4 of America's marine fisheries are overfished.

Hundreds of laws manage and protect America's natural resources.
- State governments are the primary protectors of many natural resources.
  - State law determines how land is developed and used, how much water is drawn from wells and rivers, the pace of petroleum extraction, and the taking of wildlife and fish.
- In recent decades, though, the federal role has grown.
  - Examples: The Magnuson-Stevens Act manages marine fishing, and the Coastal Zone Management Act provides for state-federal cooperation in preserving coastal regions.
  - The Endangered Species Act and section 404 of the Clean Water Act limit how various environmentally sensitive lands are used.

Suggested Discussion Questions
1. Why is the U.S. losing so many of its natural resources?
2. How can we protect the country's natural resources?
3. Should the federal government play a larger role in protecting natural resources? Why or why not?

II.   The Public Trust Doctrine

Legally, some resources have always been treated as public commons that belong to everyone and are irreducible to private ownership.
- This concept forms the core of the public trust doctrine, which provides special protection to tidelands and other navigable waterways.

The most famous public trust case in the U.S. is *Illinois Central Railroad Company v. Illinois.*
- In 1869, Illinois granted 1,000 acres under Lake Michigan along the Chicago shoreline to the Illinois Central Railroad; later, the state changed its mind.
- The railroad sued, but the Supreme Court upheld the state's reversal.
  - Lands underlying navigable waterways were held by the Court to be "different in character" from other governmentally owned lands.
  - The state holds such lands "in trust for the people" to enjoy.

In many states, the public trust doctrine has been invoked to protect environmental interests.
- Example: *Marks v. Whitney* in California.
  - Marks wanted to fill and develop tidelands he owned bordering Tomales Bay in northern California.
  - A neighbor successfully sued to prevent Marks' plan.
    1. The California Supreme Court ruled that in most cases a private owner of tidelands holds title subject to the state's public trust.
    2. Any citizen can sue to enforce the public trust, whose purposes were said to be "sufficiently flexible to encompass changing public needs."
- The California Supreme Court has also ruled that the public trust doctrine restricts the amount of water that can be withdrawn from navigable waterways.

Not all states have followed California's lead.
- Examples: In Maine, the public trust doctrine protects only fishing, fowling, and navigation; in Idaho, the public trust doctrine does not apply to water rights or withdrawals.

Some have urged courts to use the public trust doctrine more aggressively to protect other environmental resources such as forests. Courts, however, have generally refused to extend its application beyond waterways.

Critics of the public trust doctrine claim that courts are, in effect, legislating.
- The few courts that have speculated on the origins of the doctrine have held that the trust flows from common law, not from constitutions.

Suggested Discussion Question
1. Why has California been so proactive in invoking the public trust doctrine to protect environmental interests?

III. Protecting Wetlands

Wetlands are crucial natural resources.
- Definition of wetlands: surface areas that are saturated or inundated with water long enough each year to support hydrophilic (water-loving) vegetation.
- Wetlands provide a number of valuable services:
  o They help protect waterways, and drinking water, by filtering out contaminants.
  o Forested wetlands lower water temperature in summer, reducing harmful algal blooms.
  o Acting as a natural sponge, they help reduce the risk of floods.
  o They serve as natural reservoirs by storing water during rainy seasons, then releasing it during dry periods.
  o They provide natural habitat for many birds and other species.
    1. This makes wetlands an important source of recreation.

However, wetlands have been threatened for centuries.
- Dams, urban development, new marinas and harbors—these are only a few activities that have contributed to a decline in wetlands.
- In the 1600s, the lower 48 states had over 220 million acres of wetlands; less than half that acreage remains today. California and Iowa have lost nearly 90% of their wetlands.

Most states now protect their wetlands, but the federal government provides the primary protection.
- Since 1988, the U.S. has followed a policy of "no net loss" of wetlands (and has actually gained about 20,000 acres of freshwater wetlands per year during the late 1990s and early 2000s).
- The Army Corps of Engineers is the key regulatory agency.

Suggested Discussion Questions
1. Where are the majority of U.S. wetlands?
2. How are the wetlands most commonly protected?
3. What is the significance of the loss of the wetlands?

A.   *Rivers & Harbors Act of 1899*

The oldest federal regulatory authority over wetlands is section 10 of the Rivers & Harbors Act of 1899.
- The Act's main purpose is to protect navigation.
- It prohibits anyone from dredging, filling, or otherwise altering "navigable waters" without obtaining a permit from the Army Corps of Engineers.

If a wetland qualifies for protection, the Act prohibits virtually any type of destruction or alteration.

- However, most wetlands do not qualify, making section 10 of only secondary importance in preserving wetlands.

B.   Section 404 of the Clean Water Act

Section 404 of the Clean Water Act is the primary protector of wetlands in the U.S.

- It prohibits anyone from discharging dredged or fill materials into a wetland without getting a permit from the Army Corps of Engineers.
- Section 404 is much broader than the Rivers & Harbors Act of 1899.
  - "Navigable waters" are defined as "all waters of the United States including the territorial seas."
- A downside of the section, though, is that it regulates only a limited set of activities and contains many exemptions.

Section 404 has pitted landowners against environmentalists.

- Landowners have focused on the term "navigable waters" to try to narrow the law's reach.
- In contrast, environmentalists have argued that a large number of activities, including dredging, result in illegal "discharges" that require permits under the section.

Suggested Discussion Activity
1. Have students visit the EPA's web site to learn more about section 404.

1.   What Are "Navigable Waters"?

The constitutional basis for Congress's regulation of wetlands is the Commerce Clause, which has historically extended only to navigable waterways. But what, exactly, is a navigable waterway?

The Corps initially took the position that, despite its definition in section 404 of the Clean Water Act, the term applied only to actually, potentially, or historically navigable waterways—which include few wetlands.

- Environmentalists successfully challenged this assertion in *Natural Resources Defense Council v. Callaway.*

In *United States v. Riverside Bayview Homes, Inc.* the Supreme Court had to decide if section 404 applied to wetlands that were adjacent to navigable waterways but were not themselves navigable.

- The Court unanimously ruled that the Corps could regulate such waterways.

In the 1990s, the question shifted: Could the Corps regulate isolated wetlands that are *not* adjacent to navigable waters?

- The Corps originally argued that it could, if the wetlands were actual or potential habitat for migratory birds.
- The Supreme Court reviewed the Corps' position in *Solid Waste Agency of Northern Cook County v. United States Army Corps of Engineers*.
  - The Court ruled 5–4 that the Migratory Bird Rule exceeded the Corps' statutory authority.
  - The Court further stated that there must be clear evidence that Congress intended to assert the authority of an agency that interprets a statute in a way that invokes the outer limits of Congress's power.

Rapanos v. United States again addressed the Corps' jurisdiction.
- The Supreme Court reversed lower court decisions that allowed the Corps to regulate wetlands that were hydrologically linked to navigable waterways through ditches, drains, and creeks.

Artificial wetlands have generally been held subject to section 404.

2. What Is a "Discharge" of Material?

Section 404 regulates "discharges" of materials into wetlands.
- This would seem to allow activities such as draining or dredging. However, the Corps has tried to assert authority over these types of activities by broadly defining the word "discharge."
- Under the so-called Tulloch Rule, activities that led to "*any* redeposit of dredged material" were subject to section 404.

The Tulloch Rule was challenged in *National Mining Association v. United States Army Corps of Engineers*.
- The D.C. Circuit Court held that the Rule exceeded the Corps' jurisdiction.
- In response, the Corps' changed the words "any redeposit of dredged material" to "*any* redeposit of dredged material *other than incidental fallback.*"

Some courts have disagreed with the D.C. Circuit Court's ruling.
- Example: *Borden Ranch Partnership v. United States Army Corps of Engineers*.
  - In this case, the Ninth Circuit Court of Appeals ruled that "deep ripping" wetlands (in which tractors drag metal prongs through the soil, tearing the clay layer and destroying the wetlands) moves and redeposits soil and thus constitutes a "discharge."

The legal dilemma is that section 404 applies literally only to "discharges," but other activities can be just as destructive to wetlands—if not more so. Courts must continue to decide what is most important: the environmental purposes of section 404 or its literal language.

Suggested Discussion Activity

1. Have students visit http://www.wetlands.com/fed/tulloch1.htm to learn more about the D.C. District Court Opinion on the Tulloch Rule.

3. Special Exceptions

Section 404 exempts several activities from permit requirements.

- Many farming activities are exempted, for example, demonstrating the political power of the agricultural lobby.
- The exempt activities are just as harmful as other covered activities; farming is simply deemed important enough to justify wetland loss.
- Even otherwise exempt activities, however, need permits if they would change the use of the land or impair or reduce the flow or circulation of navigable waters or reduce their reach—the so-called "recapture provision."

Members of the regulated community frequently try to use exemption loopholes to get out from under section 404. However, though Congress will allow some harm to wetlands from farming activities, it did not intend to allow widespread conversion of wetlands into dry land.

Suggested Discussion Question

1. Why are farming activities often exempted from section 404? Do you think they should be? Why or why not?

4. The Permitting Process

Section 404 instructs the EPA to develop appropriate guidelines for issuing permits in consultation with the Corps. Those seeking a permit must show that:

- There is no practicable alternative to the proposed activity that would have less impact on the wetlands.
- The proposed activity will not have significant adverse impacts on aquatic resources.
- All "appropriate and practicable" mitigation will be used.
- The proposed activity will not violate other federal or state laws.

Even activities that meet these requirements are studied by the Corps to ensure that they are not contrary to the public interest (e.g., negatively affecting fish, wildlife, water quality, etc.).

The "no practicable alternative" standard has generated much legal controversy.

- Whether an alternative is "practicable" can depend on both *how* you define its purpose and *when* you look to see if there is an alternative.
- Courts have inconsistently determined the purpose of a proposed activity.
  - o Courts have required the Corps to take into account how the *applicant* defines the purpose.

The adequacy of proposed mitigation is also a key question.
- The Corps' first preference is to avoid *any* negative impact on the wetland.
- If this is impossible, the Corps will see if the impact can be reduced.
- If impact cannot be reduced, the Corps will require the applicant to restore, enhance, or create other wetlands—a policy called compensatory mitigation.
  - The Corps prefers on-site mitigation whenever possible.
  - Protection of other existing wetlands is deemed adequate, though this is the least desirable option.

It is not ideal to determine compensatory mitigation on a permit-by-permit basis. The resulting restoration efforts are often piecemeal, and the costs of monitoring and enforcing mitigation are high.
- For these reasons, the Corps has encouraged mitigation banking, in which private or public organizations work together to restore, enhance, or create wetlands in a region and use the mitigation "credits" to satisfy the 404 mitigation requirements for individual development projects.
- However, mitigation banking has some potential problems.
  - Unless the mitigation wetlands are similar to the destroyed wetlands, the same type of habitat, etc., may not be provided.
  - Because wetland banks are rarely adjacent to destroyed wetlands, the ecosystem services provided by the mitigation wetlands will be of lesser quality.
  - Mitigation banks tend to be where land is cheap and, therefore, far from towns—making them less valuable to populations.

Suggested Discussion Activities
1. Have students research the section 404 permit to learn more about it. Have them report their findings to the class.
2. Have students visit the National Mitigation Banking Association's web site to learn more about mitigation banking. Have them write a brief paper on their findings.

5. General Permits

Only about 15% of the approximately 100,000 activities regulated by the Corps go through the full regulatory review process.

Most activities are covered by generic permits called "general permits." People who want to engage in an activity covered by a general permit do not need to file individual applications, and in many cases do not even need to inform the Corps of their intentions.

The Corps has issued about 50 nationwide general permits. The most controversial was perhaps Nationwide Permit 26, which allowed the filling of up to three acres of isolated wetlands for commercial or residential purposes.

- The permit was allowed to expire in 2000, under criticism that it was leading to great reduction of wetland acreage.
- It was replaced with Nationwide Permit 39, which allowed the filling of only half an acre or less.

6. EPA Vetoes

Since the Corps does not have an impressive historical record in environmental issues, Congress asked the EPA—not the Corps—to develop the permitting guidelines. The EPA also has veto power of the Corps' decisions.
- Though the Corps issues about 80,000 permits annually, to date the EPA has vetoed only about a dozen. Nevertheless, the threat of veto certainly pushes the Corps to greater vigilance.

7. Constitutional Takings Challenges

Over the past ten years, section 404 has probably resulted in more takings challenges than any other federal regulatory scheme.

Property owners claim that section 404 has taken their property by depriving them of all use of protected wetlands in violation of *Lucas v. South Carolina Coastal Council* (see Chapter 3).
- Key question in applying *Lucas*: Can the wetlands be viewed in isolation from any other land owned by plaintiff?
  - If wetlands are part of a larger parcel owned by plaintiff, courts have ruled there is no taking because plaintiffs can use the remaining land.
  - If wetlands are purchased separately or are otherwise isolated, courts sometimes have found takings.
- Another question: Are protected wetlands "worthless" just because owners cannot develop them under section 404?

C. Incentive Programs

Incentives can often be more effective than regulations in protecting natural resources.
- Example: The federal Swampbuster program denies certain agricultural subsidies to farmers who convert non-exempt wetlands into farmland without complying with an approved wetlands conservation plan.
  - The program has been estimated to protect at least 6 million acres of wetlands.
  - By leveraging existing farm subsidies to protect wetlands, the federal government pays nothing for the program.
- Under the Wetland Reserve Program (WRP), the Department of Agriculture pays farmers to restore and protect wetlands on their property.
  - WRP protects almost 2 million acres of wetlands in the U.S.

Suggested Discussion Question
1. What other incentives could be offered to help protect natural resources?

IV. The Endangered Species Act

Most scientists agree that the world is experiencing the highest rate of species extinction since dinosaurs died out 65 million years ago.
- Some scientists think that only half of the world's existing species will survive to the year 2100.
- In the U.S. alone, about 60 species of mammals and 40 species of freshwater fish have died out over the past 100 years.

Humans are the major cause of the current wave of extinctions.
- Habitat destruction and modification are the major threats in the U.S.
- Competition from exotic species for food and habitat is a growing threat.
- Overhunting and overfishing contribute as well, though on a much smaller scale than the preceding causes.
- Pollution and other threats are also important contributors toward species extinction.

The Endangered Species Act (ESA) provides the strongest federal protection against species loss.
- It bans hunting or killing endangered species and protects against significant habitat loss.
- But it does not adequately address the problem of exotic species.
- It also provides no protection to a species until it is already in serious danger of extinction, at which point saving the species becomes extremely difficult.

Despite its limitations, the ESA is frequently criticized for "going too far."
- It restricts new land development.
- It reduces the amount of land that farmers and cities can divert from waterways.
- It constrains the federal government's ability to build dams and highways and to develop petroleum or lumber resources.

When Congress passed the ESA in 1973, it had no idea how controversial it would be; legislators thought they were passing a "warm and fuzzy" measure that protected notable species such as bald eagles and grizzly bears.

Should the ESA balance the benefits of preserving a species against the economic costs of preservation? In fact, cost plays only a marginal role in the implementation of the ESA's restrictions—which do not provide for explicit balancing of costs and benefits.

How much should society be willing to spend to protect endangered species?
- For various reasons, many people would answer, "as much as it takes."

- Others, however, think the answer should depend on how much the species are worth to humans (e.g., food, ecotourism, development of medicines).
  - o What about species with little or no commercial value? (This is the principle reason they are endangered.) Don't they deserve protection, too?
  - o Economic studies have suggested that the expected value from saving any particular species might be quite small; the frequently cited claim that many species are potential sources of pharmaceuticals or other valuable products seems to be untrue.
- Biodiversity provides a potentially greater value of immense importance to humans (e.g., detoxification of wastes, purification of air and water, etc.). Perhaps this is the most important reason to protect endangered species.
- Using contingent valuation methodology (see Chapter 2), some economists have tried to determine what people are willing to pay to save a species.
  - o Answers to these questions are challenged, however, by critics who suggest that they are inconsistent with basic economic principles—or simply serve to boost the supposed moral superiority of the respondent.

Two federal agencies are responsible for administering the ESA:
- The Fish & Wildlife Service (FWS) protects terrestrial and avian species and freshwater fish.
- The National Marine Fisheries Service (NMFS) is responsible for marine species.
- Generally, the FWS is considered by most to be more protective and proactive than the NMFS.

Suggested Discussion Questions
1. Name some species of mammals and fish that have died out in the U.S. over the past 100 years.
2. Do you think the ESA goes too far? Why or why not?
3. Do you think the ESA should balance the benefits of preserving a species against the economic costs of preservation? Why or why not?

A. Listing Species

The ESA protects only endangered or threatened species, as listed by the FWS.
- *Endangered* means a species is "in danger of extinction throughout all or a significant portion of its range."
- *Threatened* means a species is "likely to become an endangered species in the foreseeable future."
- Generally, the ESA provides the same protection for both classes of species.

Under section 4 of the ESA, the FWS can list a species on its own, or an individual or organization can request a species be listed.
- In 1973, there were 392 listed species; over 30 years later, there are almost 1,900 listed species.

- Hawaii has the most listed species, followed by California, Alabama, Florida, Tennessee, and Texas.

Before deciding to list a species, the FWS sometimes must determine what a species is.
- The ESA does not specifically define the term "species."
- Courts have generally been very respectful of the FWS's judgment on this matter.

The ESA tries to keep economic and political considerations out of listing decisions.
- After receiving a listing petition, the FWS has 90 days to determine if there is sufficient reason to order a full review of the species' status. Final determination must occur within one year after that.
- The FWS must use the "best scientific and commercial data available" to make its listing decisions and cannot consider the potential economic consequences of listing the species.
- The FWS has also adopted a peer review policy that seeks input from expert scientists. For this reason, courts have been reluctant to overturn the FWS's determinations.

Nevertheless, the FWS often faces great pressure not to list a species (e.g., in cases where doing so would limit local development).
- The ESA provides the FWS with some ways to avoid listing a controversial species:
  o The FWS could conclude that it needs additional information to decide on a listing.
  o The FWS could also decide that a listing is "warranted" but "precluded" by higher listing priorities.
  o The FWS can also avoid listings by finding that other efforts to preserve a species provide adequate protection.

Suggested Discussion Question and Activity
1. Have students research to learn where your state falls in the list of states having the most endangered species.
2. Why do you think Hawaii has the most listed species?

B.   Limits on Federal Agency Actions

Under section 7(a)(2) of the ESA, federal agencies must consult with the FWS before doing anything that might affect an endangered or threatened species.
- They must also ensure that the action is not likely to
  o Jeopardize the species' continued existence.
  o Destroy or adversely modify the species' critical habitat.
- Per the Supreme Court, this requirement permits no consideration of cost.

TVA v. Hill

- For years environmentalists had been trying to stop the Tennessee Valley Authority (TVA) from constructing the Tellico Dam, which promised few benefits but would destroy the last free-flowing stretch of the Little Tennessee River and flood thousands of acres of land.
- No law could be invoked to stop construction simply because the dam's environmental and social costs outweighed its economic benefits.
- Then a previously unknown species of perch, the snail darter, was discovered just downstream from the dam site.
   o After the FWS listed the snail darter as endangered, several individuals sued to enjoin the dam as a violation of section 7(a)(2).

The major issue in *TVA v. Hill* was whether the ESA required courts to stop construction of an almost-completed dam that had cost almost $80 million.

- A majority of the Supreme Court said yes, construction must stop no matter what the economic costs.

Congress responded to this case by creating an Endangered Species Committee (aka the God Squad).

- The God Squad has the power to exempt a federal action from section 7(a)(2) if it decides there are no "reasonable and prudent alternatives" and the action is of "regional or national significance."
- The God Squad can also require "reasonable mitigation and enhancement measures."
- Congress expected the God Squad to exempt the Tellico Dam project—but instead it unanimously denied an exemption.
   o They found the dam was not worth completing, even if the snail darter was ignored.
   o Subsequently, though, Congress exempted the dam in a rider to a 1980 military appropriations bill.
   o The snail darter's principal habitat was thus destroyed, but scientists later found other populations nearby.

What are the lessons of *TVA v. Hill*?

- The most important lesson is that agencies cannot use cost as an excuse for not meeting the requirements of section 7(a)(2).
- The case also highlights how important the ESA is in protecting natural resources.
- Finally, the case illustrates that cost and politics are realities of regulation, no matter what a statute might say.
   o After all, the project *was* eventually completed.
   o The FWS often finds ways to allow federal actions to proceed at only slight cost and inconvenience to agencies.

Because determining a species' critical habitat is costly and time-consuming, the FWS typically chooses to postpone designating critical habitat.

- By the end of 2005, the FWS had done so for only about 40 percent of domestic listed species.
- Since cost is not supposed to be a factor in deciding *whether* to designate critical habitat, the FWS usually claims that it does not have sufficient information.
  - This has caused conflict between the FWS and environmentalists.
  - The FWS is, however, allowed to consider cost when deciding *how much* and *which* habitat to designate as critical.

An important but open issue under section 7(a)(2) is the degree to which it applies to actions that jeopardize species outside the United States.
- On its surface, the section would appear to apply to all actions that do so, no matter where they occur or where the species live.

Suggested Discussion Question
1. Do you agree with the Tellico Dam decision? Why or why not?

C.   Private Violations

1.   The Prohibition on "Takings"

Under section 9(a)(1) of the ESA, no one can "take" an endangered species of fish or wildlife.
- "Take" is defined as actions that "harass, harm, pursue, hunt, shoot, wound, kill, trap, capture, or collect" an endangered species.
- Clearly, a poacher killing an endangered grizzly bear violates the section; but what about a landowner who cuts down trees that are potential habitat for an endangered species of woodpecker?
- In 1981, the FWS stated that "significant habitat modification or degradation" that "actually kills or injures wildlife by significantly impairing essential behavioral patterns" constitutes "harm."

When the ESA was originally passed, most members of Congress probably did not understand that it might eventually limit how private citizens could use their property.
- In *Babbit v. Sweet Home Chapter of Communities for a Great Oregon*, however, the Supreme Court voted 6–3 to uphold the FWS regulation.
  - The term "harm" normally means to cause hurt or damage, the Court ruled, and this includes habitat modification that leads to actual injury or death.
  - The Court further ruled that Congress intended a broad definition of "take" to provide expansive protection for listed species.

Nevertheless, *Sweet Home* did not answer all questions regarding the application of the FWS regulation.

- Example: What if a timber company cut down an old growth forest where spotted owls live, but the owls flew away before the trees fell and were not killed? Would it matter if their breeding areas had been destroyed?
- In *Sweet Home*, the Court indicated that habitat destruction/modification violated the FWS only when wildlife was actually killed or injured.
- The injury or death moreover must be "foreseeable" and not just "accidental."
  - This latter point caused Justice O'Connor to suggest that the case of *Palia v. Hawaii Dept. of Land and Natural Resources* had been wrongly decided.
- Also: Can a court prevent the destruction or modification of habitat *prior to* an actual injury or death?
  - In the *Sweet Home* decision, justices said no; other courts have disagreed, if there is "reasonable certainty" of "imminent" injury or death.

The "takings" prohibition of section 9(a)(1) applies only to endangered species of fish or wildlife. Plants are protected by section 9(a)(2). Neither of these sections, however, applies to *threatened* species.

2. Incidental Take Permits

To mitigate section 9's potential restrictions on the use of private property, in 1982 Congress authorized the issuance of incidental take permits.
- Section 10(a) of the ESA allows otherwise unlawful taking of a species if it
  - Is merely incidental to an otherwise lawful activity, such as property development.
  - The permit applicant has devised an acceptable habitat conservation plan (HCP).
    1. The HCP must minimize the impact of the taking as much as is practicable.

As of December 2009, the FWS had approved almost 700 HCPs and issued incidental take permits covering tens of millions of acres and hundreds of listed species.
- Most permits were issued to individual property owners.
- Many communities have developed regional HCPs, which reduce the burden on individual property owners, who no longer need to apply for individual permits.

Many environmental groups are wary of incidental take permits and HCPs.
- They feel the FWS often does not know enough about the listed species to ensure that an HCP will protect it.
- They also worry that political pressures may tempt the FWS to prove that the ESA can work without causing economic disruption.
- They have challenged several permits, but courts generally defer to the FWS's judgment.

3. *Administrative Reform Efforts*

To blunt the impact of section 9 on private landowners, in the mid-1990s the Clinton Administration adopted a number of administrative reforms.

- When listing a species, the FWS began identifying activities that were considered likely or unlikely to violate section 9, thus reducing landowners' uncertainties about the legality of their actions.
- The FWS also announced a "no surprises policy," promising landowners who receive incidental take permits that the government will pay for any new habitat or actions that might be needed to meet unforeseen circumstances.
    - o Environmentalists largely dislike this policy, saying it prevents the government from taking possible necessary actions to protect a species.
    - o Partly in response, the FWS has adopted a Permit Revocation Rule, allowing incidental take permits with the no-surprise provision to be revoked if unforeseen circumstances would greatly threaten a species.
- FWS also began using "safe harbor agreements" to encourage landowners to enhance, restore, or create habitats on their property.
    - o Such action, however, can make the land become subject to section 9's restrictions.
    - o Safe harbor agreements allow a landowner who enhances, restores, or creates habitat to return the land to its original condition and not run into section 9-related problems.
    - o Through 2009, the FWS had entered into over 70 safe harbor agreements, covering over 5 million acres of land.

4. *Criticisms of Section 9*

Not surprisingly, many property rights advocates have been sharply critical of section 9 for restricting the use of land and water without compensation. Their concerns fall into three main categories:

- Critics argue that section 9 encourages landowners to destroy valuable habitat in order to avoid the restrictions (since section 9 applies only to habitat).
- They further suggest that it is unfair to force a small number of landowners to "bear the burden" of protecting listed species. Everyone should help preserve species.
- Finally, some argue that the costs to society of section 9 outweigh the value of the protected species.

5. *Constitutional Takings Challenges to Section 9*

Few property owners have brought constitutional "takings" challenges to section 9 or similar state habitat protections.

- *Lucas v. South Carolina Coastal Council* does not usually apply since section 9 rarely prevents property owners from making *any* use of their land.

- In *Tulare Lake Basin Water Storage District v. United States*, however, the Federal Claims Court held that the ESA had physically "taken" water rights of an irrigation district—in violation of the Fifth Amendment—by reducing the amount of water that could be delivered to the district in order to protect two listed fish species.

Landowners who have challenged habitat preservation methods as takings have argued that the government authorizes "permanent physical occupations" of their land by the protected species, thus interfering with a core property interest.
- States cannot allow the public to cross someone's land without compensation, so shouldn't compensation be required if the ESA forbids a landowner from excluding endangered species?
- Courts say no: There is a difference between an intrusion on land by a stranger and an endangered species, which is not presumably a "stranger" to its own habitat.

Suggested Discussion Question
1. Do you think compensation should be required if the ESA forbids a landowner from excluding endangered species? Why or why not?

D.   Recovery Plans & Other Provisions

Once a species is listed as endangered or threatened, the FWS typically prepares a recovery plan.
- No deadline is required for the preparation of a recovery plan.
- Priority is given to species "most likely to benefit" from a recovery plan; no plan is needed for species if it will not promote the species' conservation.
- At the end of 2002, the FWS had prepared plans for almost 1,100 (or about 85%) of listed species in the U.S.

Unfortunately, recovery plans are poorly funded by Congress, which tends to fund only charismatic "poster quality" species such as grizzly bears and bald eagles.
- Mammals, birds, and fish receive much more funding than reptiles, amphibians, and plants.
- From 1989 through 1991, just ten species received half of all government funding.

Suggested Discussion Question
1. Why isn't the funding for recovery plans more balanced? Should it be?

E.   Does the ESA Work?

The goal of the ESA is not simply to list endangered species, but to restore their populations. Is the plan working?

As of late 2009, only 43 species had been removed from the endangered species list; nine of them were delisted because they had become extinct.

Delistings, though, may not be an entirely accurate indication of the ESA's success. Restoring an endangered population is extremely difficult.
- Perhaps the fact that so few species have gone extinct after being listed should be the best indicator of success.
- One group of experts estimates that the ESA has prevented more then 2,200 species from going extinct during its first 30 years.

Most believe the ESA could be improved.
- One welcome reform would be to protect species *before* they become endangered or threatened.
- Another important reform would be to refocus the ESA on the general protection of biodiversity rather than on individual species.

Efforts to amend the ESA in Congress remain controversial. However, easing the burden on property owners has helped deflect calls to weaken the ESA.

Suggested Discussion Question
1. Do you think the ESA is working? Support your answer.

PART IV
Natural Resources

CHAPTER 11
Energy

The Obama Administration has made energy one of its major priorities.

The U.S. has not had a coherent energy policy for years, despite the passage of three Energy Policy Acts since 1992.

Public attention to energy has waxed and waned over the years in reaction to the various "energy crises" that periodically arise.

I.   Today's Energy Concerns

Fossil fuels provide over 80% of the energy consumed in the U.S.
- Petroleum provides over one-third of all energy consumed in the country; it constitutes 95% of the energy used in the transportation sector.
- Coal and natural gas each provide about one-quarter of America's energy needs; coal provides most of America's electrical power.

The United States' dependence of fossil fuels (especially petroleum) is the source of all three major concerns about energy.
- The environmental impact of fossil fuels is a significant worry (examples: global climate change, air pollution)
- Security issues are a second concern.
  - Our reliance on oil makes us vulnerable to terrorists and unfriendly countries that can disrupt its flow.
  - Our dependence on oil also forces the U.S. to provide military and economic support to oil-producing states.
  - Oil profits are often channeled to terrorists.
- The effect of increasing oil prices on America's economy also worries many analysts.
  - Rising oil prices result from increased demand and reduced production.
  - Experts predict a major disruption in oil supplies over the next decade, leading to higher prices and probable recession.

Federal and state government solutions to these problems have so far been rather inadequate.

- Example: Subsidies for the production and use of ethanol slightly reduce dependence on foreign oil, but have little impact on the environment.
- Since biofuel prices are linked to oil prices, biofuel does not protect the U.S. from economic disruption.

Suggested Discussion Question
1. Of the three concerns about energy discussed in this section, which do you think is the most important? Explain your answer.

II. Conservation

Conservation is one of the quickest and most cost-effective ways to address each of the energy-related concerns just discussed.

Policy makers have a number of ways to encourage energy conservation.
- The government can provide the public with information about the resource-saving potential of appliances and practices.
  - Example: The *Energy Star* program, which allows labels to be placed on products showing their energy use/efficiency.
- The government can regulate the efficiency of energy-consuming products. Example: CAFE standards.
  - Since 1978, CAFE standards have established a minimum fuel efficiency for new vehicles. In 2009, President Obama announced a new program that would require 5% increases in average fuel efficiency each year from 2012–2016.
    - The federal government estimates that Obama's new fuel-efficiency standards will have the environmental effect of taking 177 million vehicles off the road.
  - Supplements to CAFE standards provide cash incentives to drivers who purchase hybrid vehicles.
  - Congress has also banned some high-energy products (example: incandescent light bulbs, which are to be phased out between 2012 and 2014) and established energy-efficiency standards for many other household appliances.
  - CAFE standards have not only reduced energy use (by about 14 percent by the year 2000) but have been cost effective as well.
- Demand-side management (DSM) programs allow energy producers to reduce demand to better match their available supply.
  - Example: Energy companies subsidize energy-saving products, such as housing insulation.

Though these conservation methods have been successful, there are some drawbacks. Consider CAFE standards, for example.
- The standards have prompted automakers to build smaller and lighter vehicles, resulting in more traffic injuries and fatalities.
- Improved fuel mileage might actually encourage some people to drive *more*.

- Increased vehicle prices encourage some to keep driving their older, less-energy-efficient vehicles longer.

Economists would prefer to encourage conservation by raising the price of energy to reflect its true cost to society.
- They advocate a federal tax on gasoline and other fossil fuels. However, such taxes have faced strong political opposition.
- A federal cap-and-trade system for carbon could have a similar effect as a tax on fossil fuels.
  - Industries that use less fossil fuels could generate emission credits or to purchase fewer credits.
  - By creating a price for carbon emissions, such a system would encourage conservation.

Suggested Discussion Questions
1. Would you support a gasoline tax of 50 cents per gallon to encourage energy conservation and reduce the impact of fossil fuel consumption? Why or why not?
2. What other current energy conservation programs can you think of?

III. Renewable Energy

The problems with fossil fuels have led to an interest in renewable energy in recent years.
- Renewable energy currently accounts for less than 10% of total energy use in the United States.
- About one-third of renewable energy production in the U.S. comes from hydropower, but because of its impact on the environment there is little opportunity for growth.
- Biofuels account for just over half of the renewable energy production in the U.S.
- Policy makers have concentrated their attention on wind, geothermal, solar, and biofuels.

For electricity, wind and solar alternatives have generated the most interest.
- Wind generates only about 1% of the electricity used in the U.S., but that represents a 1,000% increase over the past ten years.
  - Wind is the least-expensive renewable energy source.
  - Major obstacles: intermittency, long distances between best wind sources and population, and opposition from local communities.
- Solar power generates currently less electricity in the U.S. than wind power.
  - But solar power is our largest potential energy resource, and its energy contribution is expected to grow as more efficient technologies are developed.
  - Major obstacles: intermittency, impact on local land uses and water sources, and toxic substances in photovoltaic panels.

For vehicles, the major options are liquid biofuels (ethanol and biodiesel), electricity, and hydrogen.

- Biofuel is currently the most competitive short-term option.
  - Millions of vehicles that can use biofuels are already on the road.
  - Plug-in hybrids—which combine battery storage with internal combustion engines that recharge the battery and provide independent power—are also likely short-run players.
- Over time, however, electricity and hydrogen are likely to surpass the use of biofuel.
  - Pure electric vehicles need a significant breakthrough in battery technology to be competitive.
  - Hydrogen will require major vehicle redesign and an infrastructure overhaul for delivering hydrogen.

The major problem holding back increased use of renewable energy sources is their significantly higher cost when compared to fossil fuels.

- Reasons for higher cost: (1) Fossil fuels enjoy a variety of government subsidies and (2) consumers are not forced to pay for their environmental costs.
- Costs are likely to fall over time as new technologies are developed and power companies gain greater expertise in using renewable sources. Until then, major increases in renewable energy use will require government action.
- Economists and other analysts believe the most effective way to promote renewable energy is probably to impose a tax on the use of fossil fuels equal to the damages that are likely to result from carbon emissions associated with fossil use.
- A cap-and-trade system for carbon would also promote greater use of renewable energy.

Federal and local governments are promoting renewable energy in a number of ways.

- The federal government promotes it primarily through large research and development (R&D) projects.
  - The Renewable Energy and Energy Efficiency Technology Competitiveness Act of 1989 and Energy Policy Act of 1992 are two examples.
    - Economists argue that private markets do not provide an optimum level of energy R&D, so government support of R&D is vital.
    - However, both private and public funding of energy R&D has been inadequate for decades. The Obama Administration promised to change that.
  - The federal government also offers a renewable energy production credit (REPC), which provides a tax subsidy for the production of electricity from wind, geothermal, solar, landfill gas, and closed-loop biomass. Tax credits are also given for investment in geothermal and solar generation facilities.
- Nearly 30 states are using renewable portfolio standards (RPS) to promote renewable energy.

- o The programs require utilities to distribute and—in some cases—generate a certain amount of their electricity from renewable systems.
- o RPS programs illustrate the potential conflict among the various goals for reducing fossil fuel dependence—cleaner environment, energy independence, and strong economy.
- o Congress has considered the imposition of a national RPS at various times. Example: The Waxman-Markey climate legislation passed by the House in 2009 would require large retail electric suppliers to use renewable sources to meet 20% of their customers' energy demands by 2020.
- o A number of states are considering legislation along the lines of Waxman-Markey, and California has adopted its own Low Carbon Fuel Standard.
- o Economists warn that poorly designed RPS programs and low-carbon fuel standards can be unnecessarily costly and actually increase carbon emissions.
- Some states and local communities also promote the development of fuel cells, solar photovoltaic systems, and other on-site renewable sources through net metering—which allows excess energy generated from renewable sources to be sold to the local energy supplier.

There have been some dramatic increases in renewable energy in recent years. For example, over the past decade, wind energy increased by 1,000%.

But how will public policy affect the distribution of electricity generation in the future?

Suggested Discussion Question
1. Will renewable energy sources someday replace fossil fuels? Explain your reasoning.

IV. Siting New Energy Facilities and Transmission Lines

The siting of new renewable energy facilities and the transmission lines needed to carry the electricity from the generation facilities to customers is becoming a major issue.
- Wind and solar facilities must be located in areas where there is adequate wind and sunlight.
- But many of these areas are located either in regions where transmission infrastructure does not exist or where current transmission capacity is constrained, requiring thousands of miles of new transmissions lines.

An increasing "not in my backyard" (NIMBY) attitude in many communities is raising a "green versus green" debate.
- Example: Citizens of Cape Cod, Massachusetts—and local Indian tribes—oppose construction of an offshore wind farm called Cape Wind, which would furnish 75 percent of the electricity used on Cape Cod.

- The Massachusetts Historical Commission has sided with opponents and concluded that the location for the wind farm should be considered for listing in the National Historic Register because the location is "inextricably linked" to the Indians' history and culture.
- Reasons for opposition to the siting of renewable energy include visual, cultural, and environmental impacts.

Should the siting of renewable energy facilities comply with the same environmental procedures and standards as conventional energy facilities?
- Opponents of specific renewable energy projects argue that there is no reason to exempt renewable energy from the standards that apply to all other facilities.
- Proponents respond that the dangers of climate change call for quick siting.
- Responding to such concerns, the U.S. Department of Interior has "fast tracked" the environmental review of a number of solar power plant proposals.

Transmission lines raise similar community and environmental concerns as do renewable energy facilities.
- When lines cross multiple states, states in the middle sometimes object that they are being asked to bear the burden, but none of the benefits, of the energy transmission.
- Some states have argued that they should not have to host a transmission line that takes energy to another state if energy facilities can be sited in the other state.
- States historically have enjoyed jurisdiction over the siting of electric transmission lines within their jurisdictions.

Concerns over the siting of new transmission lines prompted the Energy Policy Act of 2005 (EPAct)
- EPAct authorizes the Federal Energy Regulatory Commission (FERC) to issue a permit for the construction of interstate power lines in a "national interest electric transmission corridor" where a state has "withheld approval for more than 1 year."
- FERC interpreted EPAct as giving them the authority not only to approve an interstate power line where a state fails to act, but also where a state has specifically denied a permit for a new power line.
- In 2009, a federal court of appeals held that FERC cannot override the specific denial of a permit by a state, ruling that FERC's broader interpretation would interfere with normal state jurisdiction and the state's ability to "deny a permit based on traditional considerations like cost and benefit, land use and environmental impacts, and health and safety."

Congress is currently considering new legislation to address the issue.
- Some of the proposed legislation would give FERC the clear authority to override state decisions if power lines have significant national interest.
- Other bills would encourage the creating of regional siting teams to determine appropriate transmission paths.

- Most legislation addresses the siting issue as well as how to determine cost allocations among affected states.

Suggested Discussion Activity
1. Ask students to research examples of NIMBY controversies regarding the siting of renewable energy facilities in the United States. Discuss their findings and the issues raised in class.

V. Carbon Capture and Storage

Many believe that "clean coal" can be a significant answer to America's energy concerns.
- The U.S. has a huge reserve of coal.
- Coal is less expensive per unit of energy than either liquid petroleum or natural gas.
- It appears that coal solves both the energy security and economic prosperity concerns.
- However, coal has a gigantic environmental impact. Examples: High SO_2 content, acid rain, NO_x, ozone, CO_2 emissions, climate change.

Tension between coal's climate impact and its low cost and abundance has led to opportunities for carbon capture and storage (CCS).
- In CCS, companies capture CO_2 emissions from their facilities and store it someplace where it is unlikely to escape into the environment.
- It is estimated that there is enough storage capacity in North America to store carbon emissions at current rates for more than 900 years.

CCS is still in its experimental phase; only four industrial-scale projects are currently operating.
- The 2009 Economic Recovery Act earmarked $1 billion toward the development of a power plant in Illinois that will use CCS.

But CCS raises a number of policy issues:
- How much should the government promote CCS?
- Who owns the right to store CO_2 in underground formations?
- How should carbon storage be regulated?
- How should the government ensure long-term monitoring and management of a CCS project, given that it must capture carbon for hundreds or thousands of years?

Suggested Discussion Activity
1. Divide students into four groups and assign each group one of the four policy issues regarding CCS. Ask students in each group to discuss the question and arrive at some tentative answers, which they will then share with the entire class. Lead a brief class discussion about the students' answers.

PART V
Environmental Impact Statements

CHAPTER 12
The National Environmental Policy Act

1969's National Environmental Policy Act (NEPA) was the first major statute of the modern era of environmental law.
- NEPA does not attempt to protect the environment by establishing measurable standards or requiring conservation of endangered species or areas.
- Instead, it relies on information—it requires agencies to think about the environmental impacts of their proposed actions and alternatives.

Under NEPA, all federal agencies must create an environmental impact statement (EIS) on a "recommendation or report on proposals for legislation and other major Federal actions significantly affecting the quality of the human environment."
- An EIS analyzes the environmental impacts across a range of proposed actions, considering both unavoidable negative impacts and ways to diminish them.
- Example: Before the National Park Service can build parking lots throughout the Yosemite Valley, it must first prepare an EIS on the matter—considering not only how the action might affect the environment but also suggesting other alternatives (e.g., using a light-rail system to reduce traffic).

NEPA also created the Council on Environmental Quality (CEQ) to oversee the NEPA process and its implementation.
- The CEQ does not have enforcement authority.
- In practice, enforcement of NEPA has come through citizen lawsuits under the Administration Procedure Act and federal question jurisdiction.
- Basically, NEPA cases raise one of two questions:
    o Should the agency have prepared an EIS?
    o If so, was the EIS adequate?
- NEPA violations usually result in a remand to the agency to postpone its proposed project until an adequate EIS has been filed.

Thousands of NEPA lawsuits have been filed. Why?
- NEPA educates decision makers by making them sensitive to environmental issues and assisting them in finding simple ways to mitigate environmental impacts.
- An EIS can provide a source of leverage for internal agency opposition.
- An EIS can also provide information that can be used to challenge an agency's decision in court.

- Politically, an EIS can be used to educate the public and provide information that citizens can raise with their legislators or take into polling places with them on election day.
- NEPA litigation can delay a project, allowing opposition to become organized and—in many cases—causing the proposal to be abandoned.

Suggested Discussion Activity
1. Have students visit http://ceq.hss.doe.gov/ to learn more about NEPA and the CEQ. Have them write a brief paper on their findings.

I.   NEPA Grows Teeth

See: *Calvert Cliffs' Coordinating Committee v. U.S. Atomic Energy Commission*, Supra

The *Calvert Cliff's* case was the first significant court decision that interpreted NEPA.
- The Atomic Energy Commission (AEC) agreed that NEPA required a "detailed statement" to be "prepared" and to "accompany" its licensing application for a nuclear plant.
- However, the AEC planned never to allow the statement to be read or considered by the licensing board.
- The court ruled that the whole point of NEPA is to ensure that decision makers consider environmental issues.
- Therefore, to survive judicial review, agencies must show that they have considered the EIS "at every important stage in the decision making process."

Subsequent court decisions have affirmed that NEPA is a procedural—not a substantive—statute.
- A judge can only consider whether the agency prepared an appropriate EIS; the judge cannot make the substantive decision about what to do—that is the agency's responsibility.
- Decisions stand even if they were not the environmentally preferable option—as long as an appropriate EIS was prepared and considered.
- In practice, though, this distinction between procedural and substantive review tends to break down.
    o How can a court examine if an agency fully considered the relevant factors unless it makes a judgment about the agency's final decision?

II.   When Must an Agency Prepare an EIS?

An agency must answer two questions when deciding whether or not to prepare an EIS:
- Is it dealing with legislative recommendations or major federal actions?
- Are the environmental impacts significant?

Most legal actions pertaining to NEPA have involved federal actions rather than proposed legislation.

- Federal actions encompass a wide range of activities, such as approving specific projects; approving rules, regulations, and policies; adopting plans or programs; and permitting or funding private projects.

Not all federal actions trigger NEPA.
- Example: The Clean Air Act and parts of the Clean Water Act exempt preparation of an EIS.
- Decisions *not* to act do not trigger NEPA either.
- Federal agencies that provide indirect support to local groups for various projects may also be exempt from preparing an EIS, if the action could still exist without the support.

A. Major Actions

What exactly constitutes a "major action" that "significantly" affects the environment? This can be surprisingly difficult to determine.

Agencies sometimes try to avoid preparing an EIS by dividing or "segmenting" projects.
- Example: If the Forest Service wants to build a 20-mile road through a national forest, this might be considered a "major action." But what if the Forest Service transformed the project into twenty separate decisions to build one-mile roads?
- Courts tend to ask whether the separate segments have independent utility; in this example, for instance, road segment along mile 16 makes no sense without miles 15 and 17—therefore they must be considered together.

Similarly, agencies sometimes try to divide up separate types of actions.
- Example: The Forest Service builds a small road providing access into a timber area but does not file an EIS because the project is not "major." Soon afterwards, however, it approves two timber sales in the harvest area, again not preparing an EIS because impact will be minimal. Is it acceptable to divide these actions, or should they be considered as a single project?
- Courts have generally ruled against such segmentation of projects.

B. Significantly Affecting the Human Environment

CEQ has required agencies to consider the "context" and "intensity" of a proposed action when determining if it "significantly" affects the environment.
- Questions to ask: Is the action controversial? Does it involve uncertainties? Are its impacts short- or long-term? Does it involve endangered species or habitats? Is the impact mostly physical rather than social or economic?

Suggested Discussion Question
1. What are the requirements of a draft EIS versus a final EIS?

III. Timing

Unless an EIS must obviously be prepared, agencies usually first develop a much shorter Environmental Assessment (EA).
- If the EA suggests no EIS is required, the agency will issue a FONSI (Finding Of No Significant Impact). This decision can then be challenged in court.
- If the agency decides to prepare an EIS, a draft is distributed and made available to the public for 45 days.
- The agency then prepares a final EIS, as well as responds to public comments. Once the EIS has been issued, there is a 30-day moratorium on agency action so challenges can be filed.

To be useful, an EIS must be considered before an agency decides what to do—early enough in the decision-making process so it can make a meaningful contribution.

Equally, the agency must have something fairly concrete in mind; otherwise the scope of an EIS would be limitless.

CEQ regulations require EIS preparation when the agency commences developing a proposal.

Timing also comes into play in the context of scope. Example: *Kleppe v. Sierra Club*.
- This case dealt with coal development on federal lands in the Great Plains. In the mid-1970s, the federal government had no official plan or announcement about leasing large areas in the region to coal mining interests, but it was clear that such leases were being granted.
- The Department of Interior prepared EISs for its national coal leasing program and for individual leases. The Sierra Club sued to force Interior to conduct a regional EIS for the Great Plains, claiming that the national EIS was too broad and individual EISs too narrow.
- The Supreme Court ruled for Interior, deferring to agency discretion over the proper scale of analysis.

IV. Adequacy of the EIS

Much NEPA litigation focuses on the question of whether an EIS is "adequate."
- When examining a standard EIS, courts have tended to focus on questions of alternatives, uncertainty, and new information to determine its adequacy.

The requirement that an EIS evaluate alternatives is the "heart" of an EIS.
- To address this, courts generally require agencies to consider a fair range of alternatives.

The quality of an EIS analysis is also subject to judicial review. This requires agencies to seriously address all relevant issues.

When must agencies require more research in order to gather sufficient information to make appropriate decisions?

- CEQ regulations generally require agencies to make "reasonable efforts" to obtain relevant information.
- In practice, agencies must at least consider tradeoffs between getting more information and the value of getting it.
- Sometimes an agency must prepare a supplemental EIS when new information becomes available.

What if the predictions of the EIS turn out to be inaccurate or mitigation measures are ignored?

- Generally, there appears to be no right of action for redress under NEPA under these circumstances.

NEPA also applies to international actions when they impact the environment in the United States.

V. Limiting the Reach of NEPA

Not all federal actions trigger NEPA (e.g., CAA and parts of CWA exempt EIS preparation).

However, recent efforts to exempt activities that *do* have environmental impacts from NEPA's coverage have recently become a significant problem.

- Congress has passed legislation providing exclusions. Example: 2004 Energy and Water appropriations bill, which required construction of a road in an Alaskan wildlife refuge without application of NEPA.
- NEPA has also been amended through administrative action. Example: Bush Administration's "Healthy Forests Initiative" exempted certain logging operations.

Most difficult choices regarding NEPA involve national security.

- Does the military's compliance with environmental laws weaken America's military readiness?
- Prime example: Testing of active sonar by the U.S. Navy, which can damage marine mammal hearing.
  - Environmental groups files suit to halt such testing in *Winter v. NRDC*. Though the district court agreed, the U.S. Supreme Court reversed, finding that the public's interest in maintaining an effective military outweighed the interests advanced by the plaintiffs.
  - The *Winter* decision leaves many unanswered questions: For example, how can courts decide that the balance of interest favors the military *without* the information an EIS would provide?

Suggested Discussion Activity
1. Divide the class into two groups: One group will argue that the Department of Defense should be given special exemptions from NEPA under certain circumstances; the other group will argue that exemptions should *not* be granted.

VI. Does It Work?

It is difficult to determine NEPA's effectiveness.
- The EIS could simply serve as an "after the fact" rationalization for decisions already taken.

Nevertheless, NEPA has undoubtedly played an important role in helping citizens understand more about how federal agencies make decisions.

In addition, when decision makers begin to consider what an EIS would reveal, many projects are scrapped before getting off the ground.

Suggested Discussion Activity
1. Have students read the analysis of NEPA at http://www.endangeredlaws.org/downloads/JudgingNEPA.pdf and discuss their findings.